Joe Tonks is a young and aspiring author and screenwriter who currently resides with his family in both Nottinghamshire and Derbyshire, UK. This is his first published work.

To all my family, friends and acquaintances over the years. You have all done me a greater service than I can ever repay.

Joe Tonks

GROWING WITH FICTION

A Tale of Heroes and Family

AUSTIN MACAULEY PUBLISHERS™

LONDON • CAMBRIDGE • NEW YORK • SHARJAH

A CIP catalogue record for this title is available from the British Library.

ISBN 9781398409248 (Paperback)
ISBN 9781398409255 (ePub e-book)

www.austinmacauley.com

First Published 2022
Austin Macauley Publishers Ltd®
1 Canada Square
Canary Wharf
London
E14 5AA

I would like to thank everybody at Austin Macauley Publishers for all their help in finally bringing this work to print. Especially Kay Mennour, Alexander Holiday and Jade Robertson, the names on that very first letter that gave me a chance I never thought I would get.

Excuse me if this seems pretentious, baffling or overly
spiritual in nature – me, circa some point in 2019.

If anybody were to take a quick glance at my life, my
day to day, they'd probably see a fairly uninteresting person.
In the regular sense, they're probably right – I'm not exactly
your default portrait of an exciting person, especially for
someone my age, apparently, but everybody in life has their
story to tell – experiences and memories that are exclusive to
them, which make even the plainest looking person seem far
more interesting by the road they've had to travel. I've
wanted to make some sense of the things I've experienced
for a while now and for reasons I'll go into later, have found
this the best outlet for that tale, which is strange but like I
said, we'll go into that later.

This isn't just about that though – this is about more than
just my own personal journey. It's about what's inspired me,
as well as who has inspired me. How things in life have left
only to come back around again and how in a strange way
everything, as irrelevant and inconsequential as some things,
may have been started to coalesce into what could end up
being something you might describe as meaningful. It's a bit
of everything – a reflection, some analysis (Spoilers for a lot
of stuff will follow, you have been warned) and, hopefully, a
good read.

I'm someone who has grown up with and been especially influenced by film, television and video games. Fiction and stories are what I've always been drawn to, so expect a lot of these sections to relate to various stories and characters that I've found a lot to relate to. A few of them hold great importance to me and I hope I'll be able to get across as I get to each of them, especially in just how they've had an influence on me and my life.

But before I get started, I just hope people find this at least insightful and hopefully enjoyable. Let's start with some background – some foundation to get you up to speed.

Chapter One

So About Me...

I can't quite tell whether it's me or not but everything feels different. At surface level everything is moving along just as it has done for a while now but I can't help but feel like there's been a very subtle shift in a lot of things, maybe even everything. The feeling has been growing now to the point where I don't just feel indifferent to a lot of aspects of life but maybe even alienated.

There are just too many questions bouncing around in my head and not enough answers to match. It's not that they're there already, it's that they just aren't appearing at all. Like I said, it's making me feel a little lost and alienated.

My current job is managing the impressive balancing act of being stressful and boring at the same time. I'd rather be doing what I've always wanted to do – writing but I can't just leave my job and pursue it like some wistful wanderer (Well, I could...) but then I'm running out of patience and drive to even so much as turn up for four hours, five days a week.

Find a new place of employment?

That just creates the same problem as where I am now. I've bounced around a few departments at my current employment and the more I move, the faster the feeling of wanting to follow a career in writing catches up. Is it because I'm so focused on a career in writing, especially considering I'm getting older now, that I get more frustrated or should I just be there by now? I wish...

Part of me would absolutely love to act on pure impulse and walk in with the intent of walking out but it doesn't work like that. Apart from the fact I'd need money (Not straight away, I'd be fine for a while), the backlash would be very hot to handle and make the feeling of catharsis I'd get from leaving dissipate quickly.

And so, eventually, it would lead to having to find a new job, probably in a similar line of employment, only to wonder why I'm there when I could be harnessing one of the very few skills I'm truly good at (I think). It's like some strange vicious cycle, a conundrum to say the least.

It sometimes frustrates me that I nearly always feel this way. Everybody else seems able to walk in and do their bit for five days a week and then forget about it for two days at the weekend or whenever they get time off. It just frustrates me, irritates me and feels like I'm wasting time. I know what you're thinking *but you get paid to do that,* and, yeah, I do get money at the end of the month like everybody else but it doesn't feel like enough for me. Aren't you allowed to enjoy what you do? Feel a sense of accomplishment in what you do? And use your best talents to not only help yourself gain the income to live but to enjoy every single day doing what you're best at?

I watch and hear a lot of people work at places for large chunks of their own time because that's just where they are. I understand there are a lot more circumstances at play for a lot of people but it just seems kind of tragic to me. Hundreds of people working for the money, the income and then hoping that small slice of time off justifies the back breaking, soul crushing reality the other five days make up. Can't you enjoy both?

It's part of why I've always wanted to be a writer. It's something I know I'd enjoy. Writing scripts for films, which have always made up a large part of my life, is something that's always whispered to me from the back of my mind for years now. No matter how many doubts and insecurities I have or how many other people have, those quiet whispers always prevail and pushing me onwards. I really can't overstate my hopes that I'll achieve that someday – it's a dream I genuinely think I'll hold onto for the rest of my life.

But that's just a tangent of a thought train I've been experiencing recently. There are a whole host of others lobbying for attention.

Take games for example, video games to be more precise. I love video games for similar reasons I love film and television, the creativity and artistry that goes into them amazes me and satisfies not just because they're fun to play but watching the stories unfold on screen, especially with me being a more direct part of it is something that always brings a lot of joy to me.

And yet lately I seem to have fell out of love with a hobby that I thought I'd be attached with forever. It just doesn't feel the same way playing them now. They don't hold my attention for very long and don't draw me in.

I keep find myself distracted, thinking over the fact that work is always on the horizon, whether it's the next day or the day after that and that playing games wastes another day when I could be doing something to further where I really want to be, even though I'm pretty much powerless to do so.

I also find myself thinking about everybody else and what they think. A lot of people seem to find it baffling or confusing that at 24 years old I'm not doing what everybody else is doing (We'll come back to that…) and so I end up not enjoying something I always have and probably could do if it weren't for internal and possible external forces.

It's why I really enjoy going to my cousin's house on a Sunday morning. It feels like old times when my brother and I used to go there and the three of us would sit and play for as long as we were there. When we were all there, nothing else mattered and while I get that you can't go back, I at least wish that feeling would manifest itself in some way in the present. I'll get back to you when it does…

He also seems to still get really engrossed by a game. He's only a couple of years younger than me but he still loves to just dive in with whatever he's playing and forget the time, which is the opposite case with me. That's not to say the feeling is completely gone, there is the odd time every so often in the week when I will lose myself in a game. The illusion quickly breaks though and reality catches up.

Call it paranoia if you want but it's like a feeling of silent expectation starts to creep in and fill the room anytime I let myself get lost in something like that and that I should be getting on with 'oh, you know, like life stuff'.

Social media doesn't help either. People I used to go to school with are starting to either get engaged, move into their own house or in rare circumstances, for now, have kids. That adds to the feeling I should be doing something else, which leads to worry, which enables my anxiety, which finally leads me to practicing my mental awareness exercises to avoid really wasting the day because I am unique after all, as is everybody and I sometimes forget that, which for me I think is especially dangerous.

Anyway, enough with the introductions and on with the show...

Introvert – It describes a person who tends to turn inwards mentally.

If there is one thing that gave me a sense of great relief from the past few years, it's finding out what an introverted personality is and that I fit that bill spectacularly and when I say fit that bill, I really mean to a tee.

Before I found out about introverts and subsequently researching every square inch about what one is, I thought I was kind of backwards and damaged because just being called shy doesn't really do it justice. Shy is very different from introverted and it only took a few seconds of reading to discern that I was introverted, heavily introverted.

Ask anyone that knows me and they'll tell you I'm pretty notorious for not going out a lot and finding much more enjoyment from spending my time by myself with my own hobbies than going out at weekends and 'living it up'. Well, up until a while back that used to get to me (As did a lot of things) because like I said, it gave me the impression that there was something wrong with me. Shy people might struggle to strike up a conversation but that doesn't mean they won't go out to the loud nightclubs in the big city. That's entirely different.

An introvert's brain is literally wired in a different way.

- **Introverts Need Alone Time**

This is because the part of the brain that governs social rewards works differently for an introvert. Whereas, an extrovert is energised by the rewards that come from the social scene and cultivating those relationships, an introvert is not. The need isn't gone completely – it's just that they gain their energy from spending time alone and gain less enthusiasm from the need for that reward because of that difference in their brain. It's why a long afternoon alone sounds so heavenly to introverted people. Introverts pride themselves on having much richer, inner lives than most.

- **Introverts are Deep Thinkers**

Introverts are known to be deep, inward thinkers. This is because they use far less Dopamine (See Above) and use a greater influx of another neurotransmitter, Acetylcholine. They are both neurotransmitters linked to pleasure but Acetylcholine rewards the act of turning inwards, which is why introverts are known to ponder and spend a great deal of time on ideas and tasks. Acetylcholine also influences the need to prefer calm, quiet places in conjunction with that need to be inward.

- **Introverts are More Creative**

Introverts require solitude and quiet to recharge but it's within that solitude that introverts can find and cultivate their creativity. Research has found that introverts were more likely to pursue professions in a creative field because they found it easier to tap into their imagination. (As someone who has always wanted to be a writer, I swear this almost felt like divine intervention, it was surreal).

-   **Introverts Dread (and can't really do) Small Talk**
If ever you find me struggling with 'the small talk', then I'm honestly not being rude or dismissive. It's just for an introvert, the brain sees it as kind of unnecessary. As stated above, introverts have a very different reaction to the social side of life and it can often drain them rather than re-energise them. Introverts prefer to communicate with a larger degree of honesty and authenticity and crave more deep, meaningful topics of conversation because for them it creates a much more honest connection with people (In my first round of therapy, the last two sessions essentially came down to me and my therapist discussing dream meaning and even some philosophising and I honestly loved it). So, if I'm ever struggling with small talk…apologies – it's my brains fault.

-   **Introverts cannot become Extroverts**
Because the world is made up of primarily extroverted folks, it's common to think that an introverted person is somehow not right and so often an introverted person will often be encouraged to become more extroverted because that's just who general society favours. But just like how we're often mistaken for being shy, trying to

change an introvert into an extrovert isn't going to work because there isn't anything to fix.

-    **Introverts are incredibly loyal**
Introverts don't have as many friends as others. That's kind of deliberate though because we prefer to only have a very few good friends than a whole host. Those that can call an introvert a friend or loved one can know that because introverts struggle with a lot of this side of life, we will be incredibly loyal to those we are lucky to know and trust. There ain't gonna be no backstabbing from us, we're with you till the end of the line.

I could go on about how introverts like rain because it acts like natural white noise or how we often agonise over exactly what words to say in conversation because of our more inward, analytical nature but I guess you can always find the rest on the internet (I know you're already reading this but I would greatly appreciate if people took the time to read about some of this stuff online).

It is, however, safe to say that when I found out about this on one random day, I felt incredibly relieved that I wasn't so alone in the fact that I've often preferred to indulge in my own isolation rather than follow everybody else and that I did often feel drained and exhausted after only being out somewhere for a couple of hours.

There are exceptions – I could spend all day at the cinema but I think that's just because everybody is expected to be quiet and watch the film rather than to converse and converse and converse. I don't mind going out, I often like it. It's just don't expect me to do much more than sit quietly in the background, enjoying the environment.

I can see why that would lead people to think there is something wrong with me but that is the key difference between shyness and introversion. Shyness is something to be overcome an obstacle and fear to be beaten for a person but it isn't introversion – introversion has nothing to do with timidity, it's a person's natural self and their being.

It's just a little different.

When I finally came across this information, it was my first foray into realising that not everybody followed the same path, that when a person struggles with something, even to fit in with what people might consider the normal path in life – there is often a good, even unexpected reason. I remember seeing a link to an article about introversion at the time. I had no idea what introversion was, the word had never crossed my mind and when it made mention of quiet people who prefer their own company, I was intrigued.

Aside from the article going over some of the broader points I've already mentioned, there was a video accompanying it. It was a presentation at the TED conference. The talk was given by Susan Cain, author of a book called *The Quiet Revolution*. She was an introvert herself and so in the time given described the attributes of an introverted person as well as how surprisingly beneficial they could be in a lot of environments. While the world was heavily socialised and geared towards the extroverted personalities, Susan made points to persuade people to recognise the positive attributes of introverted people.

She described a scenario in which there is a class of children and in doing some schoolwork, the teacher assigned the children into groups. It was encouraged that everybody partakes in the group work, even when one particular child felt better off working independently. Much like in business and other workplaces, the one person who was more effective in their own space was almost vilified for wanting to work by themselves. This spoke to me because I'd often been through the same situation at school. I was never fond of group work and genuinely preferred to work on projects on my own.

It's difficult to convey properly because it can seem like something's wrong with you. Like you're upset about something or maybe you don't like somebody. This isn't the case. Introverts just happen to feel more effective and even comfortable doing things themselves.

It's safe to say the presentation was an eye opener for me. Like I've said, I was often thought of as just being incredibly shy. I thought that too, that my shyness was very powerful and had a much greater hold on me but after reading the article, watching the presentation and then comparing the two, I realised that shyness really was far from the truth. Extroverts can be shy, it's a mental block which prevents people from communicating out of a fear. They still enjoy the social scene, even the louder and denser locations like nightclubs and parties, they just have an obstacle to overcome in their shyness.

This didn't sit with me because even though I was quiet, those things didn't appeal to me and so there was always a lingering set of questions in the back of my mind. Those questions were answered when I watched Susan Cain's presentation and I realised that a lot of what I liked and disliked was shared by more than just me. I was quiet for sure but there were subjects I could talk for days about, which clashed with the broad blanket of shyness. So, I finally felt a sense of relief when Susan began to describe how she, as a child and even a teenager, would spend more time reading than going out. How she much preferred to sit away from the group and take in information than necessarily contribute. I felt better knowing that my fruitless efforts in trying to overcome shyness were unnecessary because this was an innate part of my personality.

As the presentation continued though, I still felt a sense of concern. If all of this is innate and so ultimately unchangeable, how does an introverted person hope to succeed in a world that is effectively geared towards the extroverted ones. I needn't have worried, after all, Susan herself was up on stage at a well-known conference. Then she mentioned other introverts who the audience will have no doubt heard of. Abraham Lincoln, Steven Spielberg, Eleanor Roosevelt and a few more made up a shortlist of recognisable people who also had introverted personalities and went on to hugely succeed in spite of their immediate social differences.

I sat back and breathed a sigh of relief. My personality may have been a unique and less than common occurrence but it was mine and was given to me for a reason. Everything I felt more comfortable doing may yet prove invaluable to me and I could find strength in the quiet. For the first time, I came to a realisation…

That different was good.

The two most important days in your life are the day you are born and the day you find out why – Mark Twain

Ask me what I want to do as a career for a living and I'll tell you I want to be a writer, specifically a screenplay writer. A long-standing fascination with film, television and video games is just one reason why I want to be behind creating some stories of my own that people can experience.

The broad strokes of my personality would probably tell you that writing is a pretty fitting profession for me to follow as well. Quiet and reserved and much more suited to taking my time to work on something, writing is often synonymous with these traits and so at a glance it's kind of easy to put me and writing together (There's something about an Archetype in there…).

And yet, people are still intrigued as to why I chose this as a path rather than something that's maybe simpler? After all it's well-known even amongst people who don't do any kind of writing profession that it's a tricky one to get your foot in the door so to speak. I'm still struggling to figure how exactly I'm going to make it, whatever the definition of that ends up being but I think I like the fact that even though I fit quite snuggly into the typical writer role that people still want to know why I chose it because chose is in interesting way of putting it.

Starting with about October of 2008 and ending with January of 2009 was not exactly the best period of life for me. I'm not going to go into detail but it was almost one thing after another for those few months and a lot of the finer details of where I am now can be traced back to that time frame, including the first real signs within me about what I wanted to do.

I'd written before then, of course, I was in High School by that point but it was within that time that the idea of writing as something more than just schoolwork and paperwork really kicked into gear, which is strange to me because this happened when, to me, everything else seemed to be falling apart. This one idea started to gain traction and really started to interest me and the reason why I think this is where this might get a little too spiritual for some people.

Call it wishful thinking but I've always believed that everything happens for a reason, some people like to categorise this as fate or destiny and I know that others like to believe in complete free will over what we do and what happens to us (which is fine) but I've always liked the idea that there's something bigger watching out for us all.

And I believe that this idea came to me at that time to give me something bigger to hold onto and hope for. Just like the tales of old, a beacon of light in a tidal wave of darkness. It felt kind of fitting considering that I wanted to venture into creative writing (I know some people are going to read this as crazy talk but I really believe this).

And so I followed it, even if it was just a new idea at that point.

I started by trying to write my first ideas as a book as it was really the only creative writing form I was familiar with at that time. I struggled with this, however, I couldn't seem to write very long chapters. I mean they came in at about two or three pages a chapter. I soon realised I'd have a book stretching about 25 pages – not exactly what I wanted...

I didn't want to stretch my story out and I doubt I could have stretched another 200 odd pages out of it anyway. Not only that but it didn't feel right to have it as a book anyway.

I decided to wait, leave it as it was for a while and see if another solution presented itself. Almost two years later, it did.

For one of my GCSEs, I took drama and theatre as a subject. I loved film but I actually took it in the hopes it would boost my confidence (Remember, at this point I had no idea what an introvert was). For the final exam, me and another two in our class had to put on a 15-minute play which we created ourselves from scratch. As my Drama teacher told us this included having to write a script for our 15 minutes of fame. The other two guys in our group weren't too keen on doing that so they nicely lumped it with me. I went home that night, sat down and decided to look up how to write a script properly because I kind of wanted to do this properly. After finishing the script, I decided to have a read through to make sure it was in decent order.

I had a thought while reading through it – *what if I applied this style of writing to the story I was struggling with?*

I waited until the weekend and started to translate my story into script form – that was it.

After that point it was like a runaway train. It fit like a glove, writing as a book just didn't work for this story but writing it as a script, like the films I always loved to watch, just felt right.

The script I had written for our play impressed not just my own Drama teacher but the entire faculty. It even caught wind with my English teacher at the time who was also quite impressed. It was a wonderful surprise. I kept writing my own script pages at home, even taking them in to school to let my teachers read through them. It was a fire in my heart and a lightning bolt in my mind. We had begun the latter half of our teenage years at that point and school was encouraging us to look at what we wanted to do with our lives. I didn't care. I knew I still know.

I even contacted a guy in my year who was interested in camera work and cinematography to read some short scripts I'd written and get his thoughts. It was great to have someone who was interested in film like me to talk about what I'd wrote. Unfortunately, while I never pushed him too hard to read my work, he dropped contact with me after a while and I haven't heard from him since, although I know he has achieved his dream of working as a cameraman (While I was bitter for a little while, I've decided to look at the positives and realised that if he can achieve his goals then so can I).

It's been a constant ever since that day. The urge to write fully fleshed out stories in script form so that one day I can maybe see my work up on the silver screen. Nothing has compared to it for me, no other profession or line of work interests me. Is it an obsession? Maybe, but it's become such a part of me now and I wouldn't have it any other way.

Even in times when it's been bad, when I question whether I'll be a good enough writer, when I wonder whether it is even a fit for me and I shut away myself away from it, it always comes back in silent whispers urging me to write one more word and to just keep going. I really can't ignore it.

This has since created one glaring problem though.

Referring to the beginning, you'll remember I mentioned I had a job – a job in which I'm struggling to not feel bored at.

I think this is because of a variety of reasons but my passion and drive for wanting to become a writer is one of them. Knowing what I want to do means that I nearly always feel like that I shouldn't be there, that I should (and want) be doing what I genuinely love doing. A further problem with this is that, like I mentioned, writing is a tricky profession to get into and so unlike other jobs or careers where you can just jump to them, I've had to stay there while I struggle to figure out how to get to where I want to be.

There are other reasons as well, like my introversion. Where I work, it's a customer focused, hands on, fast-paced enterprise where you don't really get much chance to take your time. It's also monotonous and repetitive, although, in a way, that's just by design. Try as I might though, it just doesn't mesh.

Finally, I kind of have a romanticised view on life. Waiting for the right person rather than dating (Do not get me started on dating apps), hoping for a better sense of meaning out of everything including what I do for a living and other things which I've already mentioned means that, to say I feel restless at work, is an understatement.

It's unfortunate because I don't want to come off like the place is bad and hateful. It's really well-suited for a lot of people but because of the peculiar way I am and because of want I want to be, it almost constantly clashes with my inner self. The romantic side of me wishes I could just up and leave, say so long and pursue my dreams but as I've mentioned, it isn't that simple, wish as I might otherwise.

But I can always hold onto that hope that one day I'll be able to write like I've always wanted to. That one day something will click into place and I'll be able to turn a passion and skill that's been by my side for a very long time, through the best and the worst times, into the career that I've always known suits me better than any other.

Ever since that fateful day, it's always been almost indescribable to me, the feelings I have towards it. The closest I could honestly describe it is magic, as strange as that sounds. It applies itself to every part of me and it clicks with my introverted personality, gives meaning to my romanticised view on life and leaves me with a sense of real satisfaction every time I finish a writing session.

There's a quote at the top part of this section about the two most important days of your life, the day you were born and the day you find out why. Do I know why? Trust me…

I absolutely do.

Chapter Two
Harmony

Part two is about learning and appreciating stillness, quiet and how I actually managed to enjoy being by myself again, even after a long period of indulging in cynicism and bitterness. The world is fast, the world is busy and while that can be enthralling in its own way, there is often nothing quite like soaking in the moments when there is nothing but yourself and life's moments of quiet.

It really brings out the surreal art style of the show, it also makes it feel like an actual town, that's real. – somebody in some internet comments section somewhere

I don't have an account on Instagram but the nice thing about Instagram is that you can look at other accounts (that are made public anyway) without needing to sign up. One account I've found recently that has interested me is something called *Scenic Simpsons*...yes, that *Simpsons*.

It's an account that takes screenshots from the show and posts them onto the *Gram, The Curator* of the account is very particular about what shots go on there though. They must be still shots of, well, *Scenic Simpsons*. Shots that show the town in the dead of the night or the early hours of the morning, shots of cameras focused on characters doing mundane tasks or random household objects just sitting there. In the actual show these shots would probably last for half-a-second before something happens but on the Instagram account, you can just sort of admire the stillness of Springfield.

I've always loved *The Simpsons* as a show anyway. It's a show that's been there most of my life and still is because it's funny, smart and often heartfelt but *Scenic Simpsons* gives it a strange new light.

A small reason the show is often lauded is how well-constructed and alive the town of Springfield actually is, part of that is because the show has been around for so long and so, of course, it's going to be fleshed out but another is because the creators have clearly taken the time to really carve out the details of each building and the nuances of each character. Naturally, this makes the town feel more real and easier to relate to but no matter how much thought and effort are put into this facet of the show, it's still just a show, a make-believe town with make-believe people.

I always knew that *Scenic Simpsons* kind of blurs the line, it's a little surreal.

One image is a shot of the *Simpsons* house at night, curtains drawn and lights off. In the show it was probably just a transitional shot to show us the next scene takes place in or around the *Simpsons* house, a split second at most. But looking at it as a still image makes you think *Oh, that's nice. They're probably asleep in there…*

And then you snap back because it's a show and that was absolutely not the intention of the shot to make you ponder what the people in the house are doing at that moment.

Like I said, it's weird but beautiful.

Once you get past the initial reality bending thought, you just sort of appreciate the beauty of the pictures, the story of the *Simpsons* not being told through wacky characters and quick-fire satire but images of this town in its quietest moments.

It's kind of like real life. The older you get, the more responsibilities and tasks you have put on you and often you put on yourself, the small moments of life start to fade away. Those moments of beauty and reflection, that you only notice when directed to it rather than noticing it's right there all the time. It sometimes amazes me how many people let this pass by.

Another (animated) show that does this wonderfully is a show called *Samurai Jack*. It's not as well-known as *The Simpsons* so I'll talk you through the premise.

A Samurai attempts to stop a demon from destroying his home, in that attempt the demon thrusts him into the future where that demon rules all with an army of machines. The show is about the Samurai trying to return to the past while also stopping this demon and helping the strange people of an Earth he doesn't recognise anymore in any way he can.

I feel it's important to relay the premise of the show because just like the structure of *The Simpsons* with its fast humour and plot, it kind of relates. The Samurai Jack is on exactly the same Earth he always knew and yet he doesn't recognise any of it, not the people, buildings or landscape. And yet regardless of the fact this is an animated show sort of meant for kids, the show is often praised for the moments when the show's creators just let the Samurai sit.

Between the actions, there will often be entire scenes of *Samurai Jack* just sitting in nature eating a meal or sat by a fire. No dialogue, no music, just the sound of the trees rustling and the few animals around him. It's meant to symbolise that no matter that Jack is in a new and chaotic Earth where he must nearly always constantly fight for his life, he can find peace and a sense of calm in a small slice of the familiar.

Both of my therapists taught me the benefits of mindfulness and how it's a simple trick that would do me a lot of good. Being treated for severe and deeply entrenched anxiety (among other things) meant that my mind was working a mile a minute anyway and so the idea of just 'being right here' didn't seem to compute with me for a while.

How am I supposed to appreciate the 'now when there's this and that and this'? I kind of get it now.

A part of me wants to inhibit both of these worlds. Regardless of the fact that Springfield is just a normal town with the normal, mundane town problems and that the world of *Samurai Jack* has killer robots but in those quiet moments and still images, there's a sense of magic that I can't quite find in real life.

I can certainly try though and if anything, they've both drilled into me the healing effect of mindfulness and appreciating the stillness. Which in turn has made me feel a lot better about just being by myself (Not that I wasn't already pretty good at that).

So, in a way, *Homer Simpson* has helped me to understand how wonderful anything can be when you just sit and watch, yep.

If you're lonely when you are alone, then you are in bad company – Jean-Paul Sartre

I've played video games for over 16 years now, pretty consistently I might add. There was a time when that's all I'd do after school and, later, work. They mean a lot to me. They don't mean as much to me as film but I think that's because, aside from my brother, cousin and a handful of friends, video games have been a pretty solitary hobby for me. Film has been much more communal and familial, which might seem contradictory to what you're read so far about me but the power of sharing film with each other has always given it the edge for me and the rest of my family don't seem all that interested in video games anyway.

But as I have already mentioned, I seem to be losing my love of video games. I don't know why and it's kind of saddening to me because I really wish I wasn't. If this is looking to be the last hurrah for a 16-year hobby though, then there is one video game in particular I want to share with you.

Maybe it's because it may end up being one of the last games I play in my very long library of video games and if it is, then maybe that adds to its potency and may even give it an added sense of poignancy that is almost solely personal to me. The game is called *Firewatch*.

It's a strange and difficult game to describe because it is an unusual game that has become part of a genre that is relatively new in video games. And so even people that have even a basic knowledge of them might not have played this particular game and God help my family, who I'm sure categorise video games into probably just the two sections. Mario games and 'Shooty' games but I'll try my best to give you an image of what you do in this game.

You play as Henry, who has just taken up a summer position at a Watchtower in a National Park. The job is to protect and keep the National Park in decent condition over the summer. This includes looking out for any forest fires that might start up in the hot, dry months of summer. The game lasts around three to four hours and you play as Henry as you try and do the job he signed up for. Now the game is called *Firewatch*, so obviously at some point a huge forest fire does break out and of course there are suspicious circumstances surrounding the starting of said fire but the game isn't a tense action game. You essentially spend the entire game walking, taking in the National Park scenery and listening to the stories of Henry and Delilah, the ranger who guides you via walkie-talkie.

This new genre of game, oft described as 'Walking Simulators' can sound really boring on paper. You pretty much just walk and listen to the characters but when you're in the right mood for it and know what you're getting into, they can leave a far lasting effect on you that most other games struggle to gain. Most games want you to have fun, they want you to appreciate how good it feels to do this or do that. Not games like *Firewatch*, they have a story to tell and you're going to listen.

I remember playing *Firewatch* in late 2018. It was just after I'd started to go to my second round of therapy sessions. I wasn't in a particularly great place and thought that this game would be a relaxing and soothing game to keep my mind at peace while I get to sorting out my fragile and broken psyche. That's one of the great things about *Firewatch*, there's much more to it than it initially tells you.

Have you ever watched a film, read a book or even played a game that seems to have come along at just the right time for you? No piece of media is made to personally tailor to one person's specific state of mind – not only because it's impossible to truly get an accurate mental picture of someone but because an individual is ever changing anyway but there's just that rare occasion when something clicks at just the right time and gives you a strange sense of otherworldly perspective on something only you are experiencing at that exact time.

In *Firewatch*, you find out that Henry took up the position because of something terrible happening at home. His wife had been given a heavy diagnosis, I'm sure that whatever it is she has, it's never named and it's affecting her memory. The opening text that appears on screen at the beginning of the game paints Henry and his wife's life until this point as care-free, yet joyous. The two could enjoy life just by being with each other. With her memory degenerating though, Henry must take an increasing amount of care for her, along with the devastating stress of not being recognised by his own wife.

The stress eventually gets to him and he leaves his wife under the care of her parents while he takes up a summer position at this watchtower. He leaves civilisation almost completely behind, save for Delilah, the ranger in another watchtower a few miles away from him and a little turtle he adopts.

He drops almost every commitment and responsibility he has, completely shunning life as he knows it to sit and look over a still forest for a couple of months. In the moments when he isn't remembering what's waiting at home or talking about it with Delilah, you can almost hear the sense of liberation in his voice as goes about simple duties.

I mentioned going to therapy at the time of playing through this game and I'll be going into detail in regards to that later but one of the things I did while I went through the process of this second round of therapy is to just walk around the park near where I live. The park had always been there for as long as I'd been living at the house nearby but up until that point I'd rarely ever wandered through it. It's no National Park but it serves a similar purpose, just somewhere where life isn't as intrusive, just quiet enough. I'd love to go to one of the big National Parks in the heartland of America but the park near my house is good enough for now.

It was a peaceful kind of experience walking around this park that was just next door to me but it was also tinged with something else. I was sort of doing it on orders of my GP, not my therapist. It was my GP who had ordered me to go and take walks wherever I could to try and rebalance me and it worked in its own way. The first day was strange because as if it was my nature, I felt like I was wasting my time. I couldn't see why I should be doing it but as the days went on and I made sure to visit the park every day, I started to enjoy wandering in the almost silent treeline. Like I said, it's no

National Park so you can still hear the cars on the roads further away, unfortunately.

I also dropped pretty much every one of my responsibilities in those two weeks as well and I felt a kind of shame in it. This was an escape, a chance to get better but it still felt wrong and a little selfish to leave so many things behind to essentially fend for themselves while I disappeared for a couple of weeks. I did simple tasks to keep myself from doing absolutely nothing but I did them slowly and deliberately and when I felt like it, I sat and played *Firewatch* for a little while.

I'm not going to try and make a connection or a forced contrast with my therapy and Henry losing his wife to a terrifying condition but it was the actions of the escapees that were the same. The deliberate ways of completing simple labours, as well as being amongst nature and the power of its silent simplicity.

I used to be someone of almost relentless momentum. It doesn't matter in which description, I had to be doing something, proving my value to others but especially to myself. I couldn't sit down and relax because it felt like I was wasting time, not doing something of worth or value made me anxious and irritated.

But during my time away, when I went through an almost 'Back to Square One' reset of myself, I learned to appreciate the quiet moments and the benefit of doing things with patience and deliberateness. I learned to be productive, not busy because being busy is just filling your time with jobs just for the sake of filling the time. You don't want to appear lazy and that's fine but your mind becomes so used to finding a way to gleam effort from anything that you forget to pick your moments of effort. Everything deserves its own amount of time, even quiet.

I could have asked someone to come with on my walks, I was quite fragile at the time and I'm sure someone would have happily obliged but even after the first day that became kind of unnecessary and beside the point, I went up there for me and me alone. I went up there to remember something which I'd forgotten to learn to be alone.

It's good to have a company and it's good to keep company but it's important to remember that the first company you keep is yourself and if you're not happy entertaining your own company, you may find yourself feeling the detriments of loneliness far more than the subtle benefits of being alone.

This happens in *Firewatch* to Henry. He had his job and his wife and all the other miniscule aspects of life but when he escaped to that National Park, he had nothing but the forest and that one other lonely tower in the distance. It was back to the very basics, back to square one and learning to appreciate and really feel the simplest of experiences. He comments throughout the game when he's conversing with Delilah that he feels ashamed of leaving his wife behind while she's succumbing to her illness. Delilah reassures him at one point that Henry needs the time and care as much as she does. After all, he was planning to go back after his tenure at the tower was done.

Henry needed that time in the forest though, a part of him much deeper than his physical self needed it. Call it his soul if you will.

That's one of the great things I appreciate about *Firewatch*. It's not just a simple game about keeping a

National Park in good condition, it's about Henry separating himself from the complex workings of daily life to look at all those tiny details you would normally miss. It's what I mean when I say it came around at just the right time. Each day I'd go for a walk in my park and then afterwards I'd start up *Firewatch* and basically do the same.

It was a pleasant and calming message overall. Stop thinking and worrying about what has happened, what you might have done, everything that you need to remember for the future and just take a wander. I used to think parks were just pointless blocks of land that people went to for the sake of getting out. Maybe that's what they are for some people, an easy place to spend the time. I never realised how therapeutic they could be though, the bigger the better. The more isolated and denser they were, just like the huge National Parks in America, the more chance you would forget about everything, at least for a while.

All of this is one reason why I'm feeling sad about losing my love of this hobby that's kept me entertained for so long. After countless games, along comes one that holds meaning rather than just fun. In a strange way though, it would kind of make sense if this game ended up being one of the last I play. Throughout the game there's a slow build in the details you get from Henry and Delilah's conversations that this escape might be the last one for Henry. His age isn't specified but small details give away he isn't exactly young and so this time in the forest is as much an escape as it is a time of decision. You feel like he wants to go back but that would mean the rest of his life becomes dedicated to caring for his ailing wife and Henry sometimes hints that a part of him may not want that. Between this and the visuals of the game looking like they've been dipped in an eternal sunset, there's a sense of finality about it.

The time in the forest, as a member of the *Firewatch*, was a chance for soul searching and soul healing before returning to the world. Being alone while wandering through nature, as simple as it is, can be a more powerful healing method than some people give it credit for. It's just not the type of healing you'd expect.

Maybe if I'm being optimistic, the hobby I've loved for so long will be as enjoyable as it once was again sometime soon. Maybe I just need to remember why I first liked it, it could be a simple and seemingly irrelevant reason because as much as we all love the complex and building a fuller, more meaningful life, sometimes we need to go back to the beginning, where there's just you and those simple deliberate acts and labours. It may be the last thing I take away from video games and if it is...it's not a bad parting message.

End. Begin. All the Same.

Those of you with an account on Netflix will have probably noticed a new show on there. *The Dark Crystal: Age of Resistance*. It's High Fantasy (Title kind of screams that), with an entire cast of Jim Henson puppets. Yeah, so it's probably not for everyone. I wasn't even sure if I'd like it. After watching the whole thing over a few days, however, I think it's fantastic! A whole lot better than I initially thought it was going to be.

After finishing it though, it's kind of stuck with me, playing on my mind ever since finishing it, which is strange because while it's a great show that I had fun watching, it isn't a life changing masterpiece like that rare show or film that comes along once in a while.

So why is it still lingering?

It may have been the villains of the show, who do some pretty disturbing, unforgivable stuff (The show is meant for families but I'm not entirely sure kids would be able to handle some scenes) but I've seen worse over the years.

After some time really looking on it, one reason I can think of as to why it's stuck so well is because, to me, it's entirely brand new.

Seems like a pretty insignificant reason, doesn't it? And while the reasoning seemed strange to me at first thought too, it only then dawned on me as to how little brand new I'd experienced the past couple of years.

Those of you who are well tuned into various levels of media will know that this year (2019, depending on when you're reading this) has a very large number of things coming to an end. Film series, television series, even some video game series that have been around for years, that have been tent poles not just for me but for many people are wrapping up their various storylines this year. It's a strange feeling not just because they're ending but because so many of them are ending in such a short period of time.

This is made even more apparent to me personally because for the past couple of years (Maybe even a bit longer), it's almost been like a celebration of the past. Going back as far as I can and enjoying films, shows and games from as far back as childhood again and while there has been plenty of new stuff frequently in that time, it's all been connected to something that has always been there as a franchise and so, the past and present have become intrinsically fused for the past couple of years.

The reason behind this is probably that year long period that was book-ended with two stints in therapy, me and two different therapists working to coax out my vulnerable side and work through mental and psychological issues. During and, so far, after that I've had a lot more appreciation for everything that filled the past than before. I'm starting to think it may be subconscious self-therapy on my minds behalf to almost celebrate the better times of yesteryear. I've already mentioned the times me and my brother used to spend at my cousin's house.

Some people could view this as detrimental and in a way it's true that putting on your rose-tinted glasses and shining such a spotlight on the past might make you lose yourself but like everything else in life, I think with balance it can be positive to reminisce and lose yourself in days gone by. After all, we're constantly reminded to keep one eye on the past lest we repeat the mistakes of our own, as well as other's histories but the connotation there seems to be almost ominous and foreboding. Why not use it to positive effect? In revisiting old shows, films, games and other experiences I've rediscovered things that once brought me joy still can just as they did years ago.

Some say that we should be looking ever forward that the past is the past and we should eventually let go of everything from before but while it's good and positive to be moving forward and charging for the new, I'm starting to believe in the idea of looking at all three, past, present and future as all equal. A balance of the three (I've started to appreciate the idea of balance a lot more since my time in therapy).

When describing the narrative of the Hero's journey, the author, Joseph Campbell, describes a section called The Master of Two Worlds. This is the point in the story when the Hero manages to successfully merge the material and the spiritual when they have become comfortable and competent in both the inner and outer worlds in which they belong. While the interpretation might be a little different in this case, this idea of combining the differing worlds in which you find yourself is not unlike what has happened over these recent months after watching this series.

I spent a long time being anxious about, maybe even outright fearing the future. Then I spent a couple of years indulging in the past once I'd begun to make my peace with it. There was no middle ground, no present but after thinking about it and thinking on what Joseph Campbell wrote, I've started to like the idea of combining them rather than prioritising one. The past and the future, the child and the adult. Not just one but both working in tandem.

The Master of Two Worlds.

I think that's why this new show hit me as hard as it did afterwards, especially after spending the last couple of years finally looking on the past with a sense of warmth and fondness instead of fear and apprehension and with so much ending in the various fictional worlds I've enjoyed spending time in over the years, it was kind of hard to figure what to look forward to in the fields I love.

But this great new series I enjoyed gave me relief that there will always be somewhere to get lost in for a few hours.

A tremendous number of endings and a purely new series gave me the sucker-punch that I need to remember to not just keep one eye on what's behind me but to remember there's still the other direction to watch as well. I think with my continued appreciation of constant balance though is that each has as much strength to draw from as the other. After all, they do say that time is a flat circle and not a straight line.

End. Begin. All the same…

Chapter Three
The Three (Animated) Amigos

The three animated amigos are a wonderful trio of characters who have managed to withstand the test of time and provide me with guidance from their own fictional landscapes all the way from childhood to where I am now. People often write off animation after a certain age as 'just for kids' but that is a serious disservice to the form and as I'll soon tell you, ignores the greater meanings these characters and stories can imprint on us from kids, all the way to adults. Here's to the Three Amigos, animated of course…

To Infinity and Beyond! – You Know Who…

Prepare yourselves folks, at the top of this page I gave a small note on how this could end up being baffling, overly spiritual. Well, it could come close here.

I'm about to essentially write a tribute to a fictional character who I hold very close to my heart for a variety of reasons. I hope it links to a lot of the bigger messages I've tried to convey across this…whatever it is. So, here goes…

As someone who spends a lot of their time absorbed in various forms of media, it would probably make sense for me to have a favourite, someone I've grown particularly attached to. This is true but it took me a while to figure it out because I didn't want it to just be someone who was 'cool' or something like that, I wanted it to be someone who I could really relate.

If you were to ask anyone really close to me, they'd probably tell you it was Batman and for a while I did think Batman was pretty much the coolest character there could be. (He is Batman after all) But as I get older and I, one day, really thought about the subject, I kind of realised I like Batman because he's this really awesome, super-cool vigilante. But that was about it.

He hadn't been around for my whole life either which to me was a big decider in who my favourite character was. It was only when I realised there had been someone there from the beginning of my life and I mean from the very beginning, who I can still find something to relate to this day, which is kind of remarkable because, well, Tigger has been there from the beginning but I haven't looked up to Tigger since I was about four.

No, there has been someone who arrived in this world at around the same time as me, possibly months apart and has been here and there for my entire life. Someone who I've found something to relate to and connect with even throughout the years, some characters come and go as you get older or lose interest in whatever it was they came from but not this one. I've only just recently re-watched the first film they were in and it still conveyed something to me that could help me to this very day.

That's what I mean by a favourite character, someone who you see as almost a fictional role-model that helps you through life's predicaments with their own struggles, not just a character you like for superficial reasons.

I presume you know who it is, you *did* read the quote at the top…

Buzz Light-year, if you hadn't worked it out yet.

Now I know it sounds like I've lost it, giving an impassioned and glowing tribute to a toy (Space Ranger) but hear me out like I said I want to try and connect it to everything else and if I have gone too far at this point, I guess this is a natural point to end this.

I mentioned further back that the last couple of years for me have been a kind of celebration of the past, going back and experiencing a lot of what I enjoyed before now. Well, seeing as *Toy Story* was released almost around the same time I was born, you can't really go much further back. It is definitely one of the first films I remember watching and even as far back as I can remember watching it, Buzz has always been the character I liked the most.

I liked him back then because he was cool and funny, what kid wouldn't look up to the brave space ranger that he was (That was one of the main themes in the film) but as I've already mentioned that isn't enough forever and someone better will always appear when you're only attached in that way (Did I mention Batman?) but I've always watched the *Toy Story* films periodically throughout the years, partly because they're great but it was only after a very recent re-watch of the first film that one scene in particular hit me a little harder than usual.

There's a moment in the film when Buzz and Woody are trying to escape from Sid's dog. They've accidentally woken him up after trying to escape the house and are attempting to hide. Woody finds a spot first and then Buzz hides behind a slightly ajar door as the dog sniffs for him. Luckily for Buzz, the dog gives up the chase. Unluckily for Buzz, the T.V. is on.

Now up until this point, Buzz has believed stoically that he's a Space Ranger, not a toy. Woody has tried to tell him otherwise but Buzz refuses to believe him and carries on believing he's this intergalactic space ranger.

But in the room he's hiding in, the T.V. is on and it's playing a commercial for the brand-new Buzz Light-year action figure. Bells whistles and all.

Buzz watches on as the commercial blares about the superb gadgets packed into the toy including flashing lights and catchphrases! Buzz slowly comes to a grim realisation that he really is just a toy, made of plastic and unable to carry out his 'Space Ranger' duties and abilities. The final nail in the coffin being the disclaimer that the Buzz Light-year toy cannot actually fly. The one detail Buzz has constantly been most proud of, Buzz is crushed.

He leaves the room and stares out of an open window as Randy Newman's *I Will Go Sailing No More* plays over the scene. Everything Buzz believed in has crumbled before his own eyes.

Buzz shakes it off, however, and begins to climb the banister, hoping to prove everybody and the world wrong. Buzz will fly, forgetting what he's just seen and heard, forgetting the fact he's just been hit with a terrifying existential crisis in about 30 seconds flat, he climbs the banister, stands proud and leaps.

Buzz tumbles to the ground and his arm falls off. He cannot fly.

When I watched this scene when I was younger, it was a sad scene, little me was sad because Buzz was sad but I didn't really understand it. I just saw that Buzz was sad because he couldn't fly. It was only when I re-watched it recently that it recontextualised itself in regard to things that I'd experienced. A movie and a character as old as me were still relevant to me almost 25 years later.

The sequence doesn't quite end there as the (Thankfully) funny scene follows where we see Buzz wearing a hat and apron and referring to himself as Mrs Nesbitt and while it's funny to see Buzz in pink attire, he is still depressed after watching his whole world be destroyed in seconds with the force of a sledgehammer.

I really connected with Buzz across these scenes because as I've mentioned before, I'd been through a similar period where my entire world, like Buzz's, was essentially tipped upside down and I was forced to question everything I viewed about the world which left me with a few mental health issues of my own, including depression. It only took Buzz about a day to get over his problems though whereas it took me a lot longer.

It was the rest of the film that really brought Buzz right up to my present though. Before Buzz comes to this realisation that he's a toy, he strongly believes he's a Space Ranger. As Woody continues to point out he's not and Buzz is clearly quite delusional and even arrogant about this belief. His duties and skills as a Space Ranger more important than anything, even connections with his fellow toys. He's nice enough to them, sure, but he never really connects to them and is kind of distant to the others with his high and mighty Space Ranger ways.

After his realisation and fall, he's forced to rebuild his own self-image, forced to abandon the idea he is a real intergalactic Space Ranger and find a new way to go on. How does he do this? By starting to care and connect with the others, he accepts the idea he's a toy but he uses the awe and admiration that others have for him to lead and protect and become just as respected a leader as Woody.

The rest of the film and Buzz's journey across it was what really hit me though as much as Buzz's fall affected me by connecting with my own depression, it was this part that felt so prevalent to myself in more recent months.

See, like Buzz with his beliefs in his identity as a Space Ranger during my years of deep depression and anxiety, I locked myself away with my own pursuits of wanting to be a writer. I had to do it by myself. It was only after I spent both times in therapy that I'd realised how isolated I'd made myself by trying to one man my own belief to the point of delusion.

And yet after therapy and after my mind had been cleared, I started to realise the errors of what I'd done by isolating myself. And so (With a little help and encouragement) I started to reconnect with people, family and friends. I go around to my cousin's on Sunday's, see my best friend when I can, go out with family and friends and try to connect better with everybody at work.

I haven't stopped writing, just like Buzz didn't stop technically being the Space Ranger he used to be. They just became another part of our identity rather than the only part. I wanted to be a writer so badly, feared that by failing it I'd lose what I thought was my only strength left that I alienated myself from nearly everybody left. It was only after I went through the process of that Therapy and wandering through my vulnerable side that I realised it doesn't matter if everybody is there when you fail, as they will pick you back up. I realised I didn't need to build my strength from writing but from my connections with people.

And that's what Buzz did, let go of what he thought was his only strength and sense of identity and started to build a new one, starting by helping Woody and the other toys escape that house.

It was strange watching *Toy Story* again a couple of months ago and seeing Buzz do exactly what I'd been doing the past year. Even after all this time, I was watching a character who had been around since my beginning do what I had been doing only a few months back.

As a kid, Buzz was cool and I looked up to him because of that. Later in life, I'd gone through a long period of depression and self-isolation and so had Buzz (As Mrs Nesbitt) and then recently in my early adult years, I'd started to rebuild all those connections just like Buzz did after his fall after he learnt that he can't fly...

But, as everybody who has seen the film knows, that's not the end of the story...

As I've said, for the rest of the film, Buzz is concentrated solely on helping Woody get back to his friends and using any knowledge he may have of being a 'Space Ranger' to help others. And so, without even knowing it, when he decides to risk everything to help and connect with others we come to the climax of the film and lo and behold...

He flies.

And now, for Part Two…

Continuing with the theme of fiction spanning across multiple points in my life, I'd like to return to the subject of *Samurai Jack*. You'll probably remember me covering the show when I was writing about *Scenic Simpsons*.

What's interesting about *Samurai Jack* and how I've come to appreciate it a lot more is the two times it was present. As people who are fans of the show know *Samurai Jack* was originally cancelled after four seasons and was left unfinished back in 2004, it wasn't until 2017 when the show returned for one final bow. The show used this to its advantage and managed to weave that into its story and main character to poignant effect, especially in how I related to the show.

I went into the details further back but the main premise of the show is Jack is a Samurai who gets thrust into the future by a demon and his main objective throughout the show is defeating the demon and ensuring that he makes it back home and to his own time (Through a time portal).

When the show premiered around 2001 it ran for four seasons before being suddenly cancelled in 2004 before the story could come to a close. Jack never made it home or defeated Aku and yet back during its original run it didn't really matter as much as it would have for other shows because during that original run it was on Cartoon Network and so was made for kids. Not only did that mean there was no violence or profanity, (*Lotta' Robots got destroyed*) it also meant the show had to be designed so that even though there was a clear objective for the main character, to get home, the status quo of the fictional world had to be reset every week. It was a kids cartoon and so it would be easier to follow and enjoy for kids if every week the world essentially reset. Jack isn't back, Aku's still around, another helpless village needs saving.

And so losing the show before it ended didn't strike as hard as blow because of this soft reset every week. Kids of the time would move onto something else exciting while older fans (It was as adult oriented as you could push it) would wonder how exactly it may have finally ended if given the chance. The show and its creators got that chance 13 years later.

In 2017, the fifth and final season of *Samurai Jack* was released on *Adult Swim*. The final season was made to finally finish Jack's story and see to it that loose ends were tied up.

The show being on Adult Swim instead of Cartoon Network meant that the creator, Genndy Tartokovsky, could let loose with a more mature version of the show. He didn't just use this as an excuse to make the show violent for violence' sake though. He gave the show mature themes fitting of the story.

The time between Jack being away was weaved into the story. He still wasn't home after years of battling and so the show used this to explore a Jack dealing with depression, hopelessness and PTSD. The show also dropped the kids adventure of the week style as well and opted for a more connected storyline across the whole season which gave it an energetic sense of build-up on top of what was already there from the years spent away.

The reason I found this so interesting to me is because of how the differences in the two different runs of the show compared with how I felt and how I was.

The original Cartoon Network run was on when I was between roughly seven and ten. Much like the show, life was not without some trouble but it was still bouncy and energetic. The show reset every week and Jack never faltered in his optimistic attitude. Same with me, life was enjoyable, everything was fine apart from a few minor things here and there and every week the status quo would reset again. Nothing would change but it was ok.

The show was cut short towards the end of my childhood as I was heading into my teenage years.

When the show returned 13 years later, Jack wasn't the unbreakable optimist he once was. An old friend was back but he was cold, beaten down and in a particularly dark turn, suicidal.

I was never suicidal but I got what Jack was going through. I saw someone ragged and worn down, battling personal demons as well as literal ones and related to him. It was the same world but it was much grimmer. He was very much a changed man by the experiences he'd been through and seeing that difference in the two different times the show was on was interesting because it's so rare to see that much of a vast difference in tone and feel.

I mentioned before that my relation and love for Buzz Light-year came from the fact that there was almost a constant through line with what was happening at any given moment in life with myself. But *Samurai Jack* disappeared for a long time and then suddenly re-emerged in a very different place to the one in which everybody had left him.

I found this interesting because not many shows return from such a long cancellation away and fewer still return in such a changed form. Any that do get the chance to return usually pick up where they left off, bringing us right back into that sense of familiar comfort. The way the show used that as an opportunity and not a crux was fascinating and gave it a much more mythic feel.

I'd started watching *Samurai Jack* when it began, when I hadn't even aged into double figures and everything seemed a lot brighter, just as it was in the world of *Samurai Jack*. He was lost in the world but he met it with optimism and hope, knowing he'd succeed because surely, he must.

When *Samurai Jack* eventually returned much, much later, I'd been through quite a bit and was still trying to find a way to deal with everything that those experiences had left me with. To my surprise, Jack was back and dealing with similar issues. I expected the show and the character to return in the same way it had been left but it came back dealing with some serious adult, mature themes that resonated with me. After all these years Jack still hadn't made it home and he'd given up, even his nemesis Aku had given up trying to stop him. I related but it was still sad to watch the once hopeful hero sink into bitterness and a real depression.

I recently re-watched the very first episode again and it's sad to see the show begin with this fairly normal child who is happily living a relatively normal life of nobility in a fable like feudal Japan. Even when his home is destroyed and he's forced to leave his family behind to train around the world, he has a deep focus, drive and overall optimism about fulfilling his purpose of defeating the resurrected demon. His insatiable drive is his downfall, however, and it puts the episode into an interesting perspective when the final season happens.

Jack fails to defeat Aku in that initial fight and it haunts him. An interesting side effect of having that adventure of the week structure for so many seasons is that you almost get the feeling that you're following Jack every single day. Nearly every other story skips ahead to the dramatic moments, the moments of triumph and downfall, a story has to be well-paced after all. But even though the stories every week were exciting, it was still the same beats every week. When the final season pulled a dramatic turn and showed those final days of the journey, it really felt like you'd been with this worn-down warrior in more moments than most other heroes.

Like I said, the creators managed to use that foundation of the kids show formula to a positive effect in nearly every aspect of the story. You felt the exhaustion, the loss of hope and that melancholy. The feeling that the samurai had done this a thousand times and would probably do it a thousand times more. Him being thrown through that portal stopped the ageing process and so Jack's eternity was to suffer the same uphill battle day in and day out.

There was no way he wouldn't be broken and suicidal along with the 13-year cliff hanger that was already there it gave me all the more reason to watch because I wanted to know how Jack would deal with these issues.

The optimistic and hopeful Samurai gone, the optimistic and hopeful kid gone. All that remains are shells, feeling lost and even bitter.

I'm still working on my problems, trying to figure out how to best reach goals and aspirations that have been waylaid by the experiences and problems I've been through.

And the end of Jack's story? (Spoilers for *Samurai Jack* about to follow).

He gets up. He moves. He fights Aku again.

And he makes it home.

Choose to be optimistic, it feels better – Dalai Lama XIV

I don't know if anyone will agree but I've always found it easier to be pessimistic than to be optimistic. Maybe it's because of past experience, which unfortunately has leaned far more into bleak territory than I'd like. Sorry to beat a worn drum but I find the past has made it difficult for me to look at the future without an underlying sense of dread. Pessimism comes naturally to me in nearly every situation I find myself in and up until recently I'd let that pessimism be my default state for how I see things. Things went wrong, therefore, things will go wrong but just because pessimism is how I automatically react to situations, it isn't how I choose to be, not anymore.

It's hard work sometimes but I work my body and mind into converting to optimism and thankfully, it's starting to become more natural than pessimism. That's partly thanks to another fictional character, who happens to be the first in a trifecta of characters I relate to on a deeper level than most, two of which I'll cover later on. The first character is easily the least known of the three. The other two characters dwarf this one in cultural significance and yet, to me, he's no less important and instrumental in influencing me. Especially when you consider viewing the world in a less bleak light. His name is Sora. Sora is the spiky-haired protagonist of a series of video games called *Kingdom Hearts*. Like with the others who we'll come to later on, the character and series are going to take a bit of explaining to back up the points I'm trying to make. I've partly dreaded this section because trying to explain *Kingdom Hearts* and its backstory in any given situation is a colossal task. It's my favourite video game franchise of all time and *Kingdom Hearts 2* is not only my favourite video game of all time but has had such an influence on me that it may as well be fused with my DNA at this point. But even I'm not going to deny that it's a complicated series to explain and so I'll try my best to give you the necessary information without, hopefully, losing you along the way.

If you do happen to know what *Kingdom Hearts* is, you'll know what I mean and if you don't, well, good luck.

As a very basic premise, the *Kingdom Hearts* series is about Sora being gifted the power of the keyblade as a kid. This weapon is designed to keep literal darkness away from a variety of different worlds (That's where the Disney side of the games come in) and so across the games, Sora, along with a few others work to keep the darkness from overtaking every world as they know it. This darkness soon comes to manifest itself as a group called Organisation XIII. These guys are 13 people clad in menacing black hooded attire. They look very ostentatious, trust me, and want to gain ultimate power by awakening *Kingdom Hearts*, a long dormant world and the namesake of the series. If you're already lost, well, it doesn't get any less complicated. As the story progresses, the games touch on almost everything from parallel worlds to time travel and to cloning. Honestly, the whole thing is wild and even I struggle to grasp the full extent of the series, even after playing all eight or so games, some of them multiple times. The whole story is far reaching on multiple levels and the tone can range from *Disney* style goofiness to very serious and bleak moments.

If I had to compare it to anything, it would probably be the *Star Wars* saga, an operatic story that spans more than one generation of characters, all of whom have an effect on the overall outcome of those that come after and the story as a whole.

But instead of diving into the rabbit hole, that is the story of the games, I just want to talk about the main character, Sora. Which is a bit of a relief as while the overarching story is complex and difficult to grasp, Sora is kind of simple. When you first play as him in the very first game, he's only a kid but as you get to each main, numbered entry in the series, he grows up. In the second game he's a teenager, the third, a young adult. There are other spin off games in between but they're designed to elaborate on the story and Sora doesn't age in those.

As the main character and the hero of the story, Sora goes through a lot, he sees and experiences a lot, good and bad. His character never seems to change though, throughout every trial and challenge he faces, he has a childlike optimism that never wavers. He may come off as simple in his ways but when every other character goes through the kind of emotional growth that causes you to question a lot of things in life, Sora remains a verdant optimist through and through. Some have been critical of this, Sora ages a lot but never seems to emotional or spiritually grow. They say it starts to become harder to be invested in him as a character when he remains mostly the same.

I'd say it makes him incredibly endearing. And after being the star of the series since the beginning and probably for the future, I'd say a lot of others agree because while he's often childlike and light-hearted in even the bleakest of situations, he never comes off as immature. There's one moment in the second game where his best friend pours out his heart and soul to him after he basically abandoned him. Sora responds by pulling a funny face rather than come off as emotionally detached. It helps deflate the situation and Sora gives him a hug afterwards, proving he was listening. He's just a grown-up kid, full of simple gestures.

Other characters, good and bad, often question why Sora was chosen. The keyblade apparently chooses who wields it, choosing worth and spirit over physical strength but while other characters often struggle with reason and the consequences behind their decisions, Sora just does what he thinks is right and what's good. It's kind of a hokey, Disney-esque message that just doing what is right will automatically win the day but Sora doesn't always win, not straight away anyway but the constant intention to do what's good and only good is what I think makes him so endearing and even inspirational. He doesn't have incredible technology or immense physical strength, just a big heaping of goodwill and an impenetrable smile.

The conflict of the games is universal in size and scope, characters are fighting to protect entire worlds from life ending consequences, whereas those that are on the side of bad want to attain unlimited power. Sora just wants to get home – a home he was taken away from in the very first game. Whereas everybody else wants something much bigger than themselves. Sora just wants that simple pleasure of being with his friends on his island home.

Sora is a refreshing character for me, other characters come into their own by learning to be more adult to appreciate and reconcile with the gravitas and responsibility of what they're doing and trying to accomplish. They're fantastical characters but they often grow into the most protective and self-serious heroes. Sora doesn't, he learns and observes the world around him like anybody else but he never loses his childlike wonder and temperament but while it would be easy to criticise the character and his design for, essentially, never growing, the game makes a pretty compelling point that, sometimes, that kind of person is often what others need.

Sora, as a character, knows this. He isn't letting go of his bouncy attitude because he's reluctant to. It's because he knows that in a wide cast of characters with self-serious objectives, overshadowed by an impossible sense of gravity, they all need someone who can appear at any time with a wink and smile. One of the series' many themes is why Sora was chosen by this unique object and as the games go on, you start to see why. It's because he's such a pure person, guided by the ideals of friendship, positivity and his own optimism.

Before I go on a little bit of history about two of the entries in the series. As I've mentioned, the main entries are where the bulk of the story happens, the big moments and weighty revelations all happen in the main, numbered entries and so these are much more anticipated by default than the spin-offs we get in between. Anybody who knows about

Kingdom Hearts will know of the notorious gap between the second and third numbered games. The wait was almost 13 years.

For a series that is known for its overarching story that continues to build, 13 years is an excruciating amount of time to wait. *Kingdom Hearts 2* was actually the first game I played in the series back in 2007 – a year after it was released. Back when I played it, I was only 12 years old, had only moved up to secondary school and had yet to experience a lot of the painful memories I remember from the years that followed. As a big fan of the second game, I was among the folks who had to wait well over a decade for that coveted third entry. When it finally arrived in early 2019, well, I've already been over what I'd been through and experienced...

The anticipation only built further when the team behind the games billed *Kingdom Hearts 3* as a conclusion to a lot of the story threads that had been introduced and built over the long years between the two main entries. It was a rare instance where the target audience had grown with the characters in the game.

When I played the second game in 2007, Sora was almost the perfect avatar for me as a 12-year-old. His bouncy, optimistic attitude fit most 12-year-old boys and therefore made him easy to relate to and to like. By the time we had reached the third game, another twelve years later, I almost expected Sora to have changed with me. I barely remember what it was like being twelve-year-old me and so I just assumed that because I latched onto Sora so easily back then, that he'd be similar to an aged me. But as those who are critical often mention, Sora never changes.

Sora happened to be exactly the same as where everybody had left him. He'd aged, just like everybody else, but regardless of the looming apocalypse that he and you the player, had to somehow stop, he was still the exact same joyous, light-hearted kid that everybody loved. One section of the third game sees you visit a world that you visited in the second game all those years ago. As Sora and friends enter, the same melody plays in the background that once did and the sense of grin inducing nostalgia is almost overwhelming. It felt like a homecoming, which, to be honest, sums up 2019 as a whole. I'll go over it in more detail further on but after everything that's happened and especially what I've done over the couple of years before it, 2019 feels like a return to something a little better or at least the start of it. And there was no better way to start that homecoming than to come back to something that gives me the warmest feeling.

A big part of that feeling is Sora himself. It's very rare for a character in a long running series to stay the same. An audience will usually get bored of the character if they don't but Sora never did. Sure, there's probably some nihilistic argument to be made that, just like the Disney Worlds that make up the bulk of the game, Sora not changing is meant to give you those warm, fuzzy feelings of nostalgia so you like the whole thing more but who cares when the world seems to be turning into a more cynical, twisted place, someone who treats every situation with a smile and a kind of naivety might be just what everyone needs.

I know I did. After finally coming out of therapy and that sinking abyss that are my mental health issues, I was sort of at a loss. I'd definitely conquered some horrible habits of constantly feeling dread and hopelessness but even after getting treatment, it was hard not to see where I was now and not have felt cynical and bleak about the situation. When you're so used to living with those feelings, you forget how much time is passing and how much has already passed. So, when I finally came to a breakthrough with my treatment, I only then noticed how much older I'd gotten and how much further back my childhood felt.

I at least had the third *Kingdom Hearts* game to look forward to though. I'd waited years for it after all. But seeing as, at the time, it was meant to be a conclusion, I assumed I'd see the story end and then be left to figure out what to do. Funny thing is, when the game's story finally finished, it very clearly wasn't the end. Some loose threads were tied up for good but the story and the characters were all left in a place where we'd definitely soon be returning. And between that and Sora staying characteristically the same, it was the first answer in what I'd have to do next or at least where to begin again.

One of my favourite things about Sora as a character is that he never really let go of his sense of childhood. He ages, he grows and he learns about the intricacies of the world around him just like his friends but he never let go of that innocence and naivety that makes up childhood. It's easy to brush him off as immature and as someone who's unable to truly comprehend the gravity of his situation but that's Sora's greatest trait and his gift. The experiences and events of life, of anybody's life, can chip away at your emotional core and your spirit, it becomes easy to develop a thick skin that can seem cynical, even if you're still a nice, good person. But surely there's a great strength in matching life's

63

challenges with an unbreakable optimism that is summoned straight from your younger self – someone who only appreciated the simple pleasures.

It made the third game so much more special than it would have probably already been. I'd kind of reached the end of one painful road and heading into 2019 I didn't quite know how to feel. How was I going to match the new challenges that would surely await now that I'd started to reintegrate with the world proper?

If someone's horrible to you, give them some humour and a smile. If you fail at something, just give it another go. Remember to take care of everybody, especially your friends and family and remember that there is something interesting and fascinating about everything. Everybody needs to grow to learn about their place in the world and how to take care of themselves but who said you had to let go of your childhood to do that?

This game came right when I needed it. The fact that the story wasn't really over once the credits rolled was a pleasant surprise on top of the strangely and timely epiphany I got from playing it. I got the idea that because this was, apparently, the big conclusion to the story I'd waited since I was 12 to see end that it would be time to move on afterwards and wave goodbye but the story didn't end and it showed me that neither does everything have to end. Its stories and characters like this, where I find my strength and my inspiration, and I started to understand and appreciate Sora as a character a lot more once I'd played the third game with many years of life experience behind me. He's someone who is so connected with his childhood self that he can find all the strength he needs from the optimistic and wondrous younger self he used to be. It's why he's the hero of the series and a character I hold in especially high regard now more than ever. His shining compassion, courage and sheer blinding optimism are rooted firmly in his childhood. A place that many seem fit to forget or toss aside but that's the thing about childhood and its simple pleasures.

Sometimes they are the greatest strength of all.

Chapter Four
Trauma and Identity

Everybody goes through trauma – it's a part of life and everybody will come across some of it eventually. Some of it is of the universal kind, like death in the family but sometimes a person can experience what they think might be more than their fair share and it can absolutely affect them in a myriad of ways. I'll tell you about mine, how I dealt with it initially and how I (hopefully) overcame it. I'll also go over how it's changed my identity and what I've built from that destruction, as well as how two heroic characters helped to understand that change and just how far we can take our identity when it's been broken down.

Remember Who You Are

I don't know if anybody reading this has ever watched *Les Misérables*, stage play or film. I tried to watch the film but couldn't get into it (Interesting fact – it's the only film I've never finished, I've even sat through all of *Batman and Robin*).

Even if you haven't seen either version, I'm sure you're familiar with the history behind its story – the French revolution when it comes to revolutions, that one is up there. The French people, finally sick and tired of the ruling elite hogging everything from currency to food, decide to really go ham on them all and do whatever they can to change things. Proper Revolution.

But that's revolution in a nutshell, right? One party is sick of relaying the same desperate message for the umpteenth time to another (Usually more prosperous) party that just won't listen. As much as they are bloody and tragic affairs, there is a degree of romanticism to them in their broad stroke events. Hmmm...

Right. Suppose I should address the elephant in the room. I'm sure you've noticed it pop up at quite a few points. Mainly because the events surrounding it have quite substantially influenced my life.

In the span of about one year, I went to therapy twice. Both sessions with separate therapists bookended this time span of about a year. The primary reasons were diagnosed down to being moderate depression and severe anxiety and maybe some other things that weren't entirely confirmed. There's an argument to be made that maybe I should've never needed to go if I hadn't buried some things for nine years between the events in question and the first round of therapy was around.

I'm not going to go into detail as to why I went other than it wasn't just for the initial events that happened many years ago but also for another event that happened a lot more recently (Early 2014), one which absolutely destroyed me emotionally but, in hindsight, may have set me on the path back to somewhere a lot better.

But enough of that, like I said, I spent some time in therapy mainly because I'd had enough of feeling off and down. Why then? Why nine years later? God only knows, I've mentioned divine intervention before, so you never know…

And in that first round of therapy, it was like the traditional therapy you always imagine and see on T.V. minus the lying back on a therapists sofa. Lots of talking, lots of digging and getting to the bottom of whatever was lurking in my conscious and subconscious mind. Luckily, I knew what I was getting into before I went so when things got rough (They do, I doubt that kind of thing would work if it didn't at some point) I was at least primed and ready.

It felt good though, as much as it can be a hard medicine to swallow. I was relieved I was finally getting a professional to help me with some dark, yet vulnerable parts of me that had almost taken over. And so, for about eight or so weeks we chipped away and got to the root of some of these problems, finding causes, solutions and reasons. After eight weeks, I thanked my therapist, we shook hands and I left satisfied with the work we'd done. It was all over.

Ha, stupid me.

It was a sunny and warm bank holiday. Some time had passed and it was the following year. I'd recently changed department where I was working and I was out with family and friends drinking.

The day rolled on. We wandered the local drinking establishments having a drink in each. We were all getting a little tired and maybe a little tipsy. Everybody gathered at our final destination of the day and we all sat down with a drink. For some reason (I'm not going into details) things got a little tense and I suddenly flipped.

Sorry, I can do better than that.

I went furiously berserk.

It was apparently quite the sight to behold a terrifying sight. I leapt up screaming at an entire group of people, knocked back my chair and started to slam my clenched fists into the nearest table.

This was a public place. A full, brimming pub.

I was then calmly led outside and began to sob, partly because of shame as to what I'd just done and for a lot of other reasons. It was pretty much a full blown mental and emotional breakdown.

After that day, I noticed, even though I had only just moved to a new department, I was already feeling bored and miserable. I couldn't quite concentrate on anything, not at home or at work. One round of therapy clearly hadn't been enough and so after some thought, I decided I was going to have to give them a call and set up more sessions. This wasn't finished.

Well, after a second assessment (Not sure why I needed that) and some moving around here and there, I was finally given a new therapist. New building and everything. The previous therapist I had was at the local GP practitioners while this one was in a fancy private building. It was quite nice actually. The first session went just as the past ones had – a lot of talking and digging but the following five sessions were very different.

I was diagnosed with moderate depression and severe anxiety before I went to even the first therapist and so they already knew what to look for even before they'd met me.

The first therapist I had seemed to focus in on the depression side, especially because of how they worked, digging up the past events that had caused my trauma. The second therapist, however, focused almost entirely on the severe anxiety part of my diagnosis and so used a whole mental toolbox of techniques to try and help.

From physical exercises to mental exercises to emotional exercises, there was entire booklets they gave me to try and combat my own severe anxiety because as they mentioned, I had severe anxiety, you don't beat that, you just fight it day in and day out. I still do and it can be very hard work sometimes. I even took some time away from work to get it done properly this time. At the time of going, I was kind of annoyed that I had to go again for something that I presumed I was rid of but you know what they say about hindsight (Wonderful thing, so forth, so forth…)

Looking back though, the entire year, bookended by the two sessions in therapy was something of a crucible for me. I'd almost like to think of it as a spiritual journey if that didn't sound kind of ridiculous and that includes the breakdown because in a way that was the connective tissue between the two. There's an argument to be made that because I had a breakdown and had to go to therapy again the first round didn't work. But I disagree, the first round did its job just as it should of, in a way.

I assumed the first round would fix the problems I had. My first therapist took what was blanketing my mind and saw the low moods, the depression. They made me look directly at my vulnerable side, showed me those terrifying, near unstoppable demons at the very bedrock of my heart and soul and between us we managed to pretty much purge one of them from my system – one of them because as I've mentioned, there were two and one of them is probably latched on for life. Between them, they were around for too long without me addressing either one. You can heal most wounds but there will always be scars. There was even some talk of there being some kind of low-level PTSD. That one will remain a mystery though…

Luckily, anxiety seems to be a little bit simpler to deal with than depression. Not necessarily easier but the techniques in battling it are there and have, so far, proven effective in keeping it mostly at bay but it isn't easy and there are still some days when it can be a little overwhelming. At least those days are less frequent these days.

What do you mean where's this going? Fine, I'll get to the point.

As I've thought on that year, I've often had a negative outlook on the breakdown. I'm ashamed of what I did on that day and often wish I hadn't if I could have. But you know what they say about clouds (Silver linings, so forth, so forth…) and after looking into breakdowns and the why's surrounding them. And a big breakdown like the one I had has been likened to a revolution of the brain.

Aha, that talk of *Les Mis* was leading somewhere!

It's almost like the subconscious parts of your brain are sick of the conscious parts of your brain doing what it's doing. Because even though it may not seem like it, you're, deep down, harming yourself with day-to-day habits or procedures. You've led yourself astray from who or what you really are at your core and well, your brain just isn't going to take it anymore!

And so, snap. Your brain decides it's best to blow all the fuses and give you some serious medicine. It's tried to tell you, tried to send you signals but for some reason you're not listening and so drastic measures are required, collateral damage be damned.

I was living with a variety of untreated mental health problems for a very long time, nearly nine years and because of a few different reasons I decided it was best to bury it all and leave it untouched. Don't ever do that because anxiety and especially depression don't just exist in you, they fester and consume you until you pretty much become a shell of your former self. When you're living with those kinds of things for that long, untreated, the person you love and trust the least of all is yourself. You hate yourself, can't stand to look at yourself in the mirror. And so, inevitably, at the age I was, you start to look exclusively at outside forces for inspiration and a sense of direction.

Now there is nothing wrong with looking to outside forces for some growth in your life (Did I mention balance yet?) but to look exclusively at them restricts yourself because you start to lose sight of you at what's at your core and subconscious. And I think that's what happened with me. Years of mental health problems left me completely detached with myself and what I wanted, why I wanted. I didn't notice it for a long time because depression and anxiety had warped my heart and mind and so when I went to that first round of therapy and we started to take cracks at them both, that's when my subconscious started to take note.

And I think that's why I had that breakdown. Between the first round of therapy, the breakdown and then the second round of therapy, it was all one long process of healing, of coming back to life essentially. The first round of therapy didn't fix me, it reset me. I noticed after I'd finished going through that first round, I felt empty. I'd lived with those problems for that long, that's all there was in there. And a vacuum must be filled, physics and all that. So for a while I lived with nothing but emptiness, I'd done some therapy and all was well.

But I couldn't just live as I had done when I was living with these illnesses so my mind did what it could to tell me that but in the end it had to resort to a full-on assault to slap me awake. The breakdown and a revolution of the subconscious mind. The void had to be filled.

And not just with what everyone else was doing but with what was fulfilling and meaningful to me, to my own heart, mind and soul because as the breakdown showed me, it had been far too long…

One particular example that showed me this difference in my own self came just before I went for my second round of therapy. A few people had come to note that maybe the reason I was miserable at work was because I didn't do as many hours as I used to. I only work 20 hours where I'm employed because I also want time to do, well, this. But I used to do a lot more, I mean there was a long period where I would take anything that was going. Six days, above 40 hours, it was masochism (Money was coming in though).

It was a genuinely interesting and quite puzzling question. It took me a good while to figure out why that was because even at that time I was in agreement. How come I didn't used to mind working ridiculous hours back then?

I think I know why and my instinct feels pretty strong on it too (Instinct. An old friend I've dearly missed) I used to work all those hours before I even considered going to therapy. I didn't care about myself, my goals, I just followed the crowd. I only started to drop my hours when I realised I had other goals and aspirations and that maybe I'd need to sacrifice some of those hours to get there.

It was a strange catch 22. Live with depression and anxiety, let them take hold and make me hate the sight of myself and I wouldn't care how long I worked, how exhausted it made me but then go to therapy and beat back those demons and I'd realise that I didn't want to do the normal, the banal. On one side the money was a lot better but on the other, I wasn't myself.

I know and understand why some people might think I'm being lazy, shunning my responsibility to the workplace and the others I work with but I just can't do it. The more I get better and feel better, the more I believe in my aspirations and feel pride in the skills I might be able to make use of, the more I lose any interest in where I currently am if there was anything to begin with.

Funny thing is, right before I decided to make the trip down to the doctor's for that initial diagnosis, I remember worrying that whatever treatment I would end up taking for my then unknown mental health problems, that it would change me. I wanted to be cured but not changed. Looking back, that was absolutely the depression talking.

I did and at the same time didn't. That long and interesting year wasn't just a curing process but a rebirthing process. I've mentioned something about it in every section before this one. Between remembering the things I enjoyed in the past to those things finding new life in the present, the therapy sessions and breakdown didn't just cure me. It galvanised my identity and balance. I feel better about the things I like and even the things I still don't have because maybe I'm not meant to just yet. I felt proud of my introverted personality, even though we're very much outnumbered and also realised that because I was such an insular person at heart, maybe that's why my depression and anxiety hit so hard.

At the very beginning I said that 2019 had been a strange year because it felt like everything had changed and I was a little alienated from everything. It almost feels like this year has been one where I've finally stopped and have been given the chance to reflect on everything that has happened up until this point (Did I mention my sudden affair with the past?) It hasn't been a particularly eventful year for me personally but I'm good with that.

I've actually been able to appreciate the past for it's good and bad and maybe look forward to a future that seems hopefully brighter. But I don't know that, no one does.

But thinking back on all that's happened, especially with the recent year I've just written about, that immortal, 25-year-old line feels more important and meaningful than ever…

Remember who you are.

The value of identity, of course, is that so often with it comes purpose – Richard Grant

I am Iron Man.

The end of the first *Iron Man* film sees Tony Stark speak these words in front of a gathered crowd of reporters. Usually in a Superhero film the hero in question is forced to struggle and work to keep their identity a secret. It's an easy source of conflict for a film to explore and to generate tension with.

Tony Stark, however, throws that completely out of the window when he lets the words loose on live television. He is Tony Stark after all, confident, remarkably intelligent and with a quip for everything anyone says. At least that's what the outside appearance would tell you because at the beginning of the first *Iron Man* film that's all that Tony Stark is. That's what encompasses every part of his identity. They sound like good character traits for a person to have but then they also come with arrogance and an air of pomposity. With these traits, his massive monetary income from being a weapons manufacturer and everything else that Tony Stark is and has, he is essentially invincible at the start of the film, albeit socially invincible. And yet you get the idea that he sees himself as almost literally invincible, that nothing on Earth can touch him. He's even taking selfies with the soldiers in the military convoy he's riding in.

Then the convoy is assaulted by terrorists. The soldiers are all killed in quick succession and Tony Stark is left with a load of shrapnel in his body from an explosive made by his own company. It should have killed him but the terrorists drag him back to their hidden base and a captured doctor revives Tony by fitting a car battery to his heart. Most of the shrapnel is removed but not all of it, he'd die if it was all removed.

The terrorists demand Tony builds them weapons of their own with the captured Stark equipment they have but Tony secretly builds a metal suit of armour to use so that he and the doctor can escape, as well as a miniature 'Arc Reactor' to become his new heart.

That moment where Tony almost dies when he's alone in the desert with shrapnel lodged in his chest changes Tony's life. That massive invincibility he felt is destroyed in an instant and as he sits in that small cave with only the doctor for company he's forced to, quite literally, re-forge his identity as a person. The very thing he's built his entire life around has almost killed him.

When Tony finally escapes the cave in the first armoured suit he'll wear, he's a changed man in more ways than one. His worldview has been shattered through the traumatic events of his time in the dark cave and he understands it's time to change. The doctor unfortunately dies helping Tony escape but not before urging Tony not to waste his life. After all, it's a miracle he's even still alive to attempt an escape.

Tony destroys the camp and the terrorists occupying it before jetting off in his suit leaving nothing but a fiery wreck behind where the mountain camp was. The terrorists had given Tony a traumatic, life changing event but he deals with it by annihilating them and flying high and above the terrain.

It's one way of dealing with it, I guess.

For the remainder of the first film and its sequel, Tony fights terrorists and other forces similar as he perfects his suit and deals with the aftermath of his homecoming, he struggles in his fight but succeeds in the end because nothing on Earth can match the Invincible Iron Man. The trauma of the cave may have shook Tony's identity but it doesn't take too long for him to rise above it and change accordingly. He's no longer socially invincible and takes a bit more care in the people close to him but the arrogance is still there in a way and he now has a high tech, flying suit to compensate for his internal changes.

He shuts down his weapons company, deciding if he's going to help people and save the world, then he's going to do it himself with the same technology and know how he used to get out of that cave. The cave is an important part of Tony Stark's journey because it's the moment Iron Man is born or should I say forged. The actor behind Tony Stark, Robert Downey Jr., has spoken before about how everybody must find their way out of their own cave. At some point in life a lot of people will surely have a moment where they find themselves lost and need to pull themselves back and leave their cave, which is probably going to be a figurative cave for most.

But while the cave is the moment Iron Man is born, I personally don't think that's the most important moment for Tony Stark that comes later.

Fast forward to the events of *The Avengers*. New York is under attack from a seemingly endless army from a portal above the city. The Avengers fight back but the military decide it would be better to send a nuclear missile to New York and destroy it. The characters pretty much all agree that that's a bad idea but the missile is already on its way. Nobody has any idea what to do until Tony decides to take hold of the missile while it's still in flight and guide it into the portal and into space where the attacking fleet is waiting.

Of course, Tony must do this on his own. He's the Invincible Iron Man after all, nothing so far has been able to defeat him. So he flies the missile through the portal and lets it loose towards the massive fleet awaiting but not before he gets a good long look at space and the alien fleet on the other side. That's when it really sets in that this may have been a one-way trip. Luckily, he falls back through the portal just before it closes and survives. The experience of seeing what was on the other side though gives Tony his second big traumatic event, one that is arguably more powerful than the first. The cave changed Tony but he was able to take a hold of that change and use it to his own benefit.

But the vast space and the subsequent fleet waiting on the other side showed Tony the infinite possibility and danger of the universe and that no matter what he did or what he built, he can't prepare for everything out there. He can't defend Earth against everything because he can't predict everything. The rest of his journey across the *Marvel Cinematic Universe* (we see Tony for another six films) sees him really trying though and because of this, he is deemed The Futurist.

A Futurist or futurologist is a term used to describe scientists or social scientists who dedicate their life and work to predicting and hopefully preventing as many scenarios as possible to be prepared for everything possible. After his second traumatic event, Tony embodies this term by building more suits of armour, then a legion of robots, then signing a government accord to contain the actions of superheroes like himself and so on…

These never end up going well and cost Tony physically, mentally and emotionally. He loses friends and allies and gains anxiety and PTSD from his trip into outer space. And yet he does this all in the name of protecting Earth from what might come from the great beyond and eventually destroy everybody. The trauma of the cave showed Tony he wasn't invincible and the trauma of the wormhole into space showed Tony that Earth wasn't invincible. These two events coalesce and drive Tony and his life going forward, not exactly in a positive way.

Tony is still Iron Man but he's also The Futurist. He must prepare for every possible danger because the cost will be too great if he doesn't, he can't even bear to think about it. He runs off in an anxiety ridden panic if he does. He declares at the end of the first *Iron Man* film that he is Iron Man because that sense of social invincibility had transferred into an almost physical invincibility with his new suit. Now he doesn't even have that. Only the possibility of what might destroy him and by extension, everybody else.

There's a film analyst I like to watch, his name is Leo Dryden (His channel on YouTube is called *Implicitly Pretentious* if anyone is interested) and while watching one of his recent videos he noted something interesting about trauma. I'm probably para-phrasing a bit but he said that "Trauma contradicts a person's worldview and core beliefs to the point that it destroys their sense of continuity." I found this interesting because it makes a lot of sense. The Traumatic event, whatever it may be, affects you so much that you can no longer see a fluid future or timeframe. You only focus on the trauma and how you can prevent it or change it. There's no longer a sense of 'the future' because your mind becomes determined to solve the problem of the trauma, it didn't match what you knew so it must be corrected.

There's a good reason I've spent a lot of time writing about Tony Stark. Between him, Buzz and Sora, they form a strange Trifecta of characters who have become kind of linked in a way, linked with me. In their actions and the events, they go through I've found something deeper to relate with them. I've gone over Buzz and Sora already but Tony Stark and his identity as Iron Man and The Futurist is what I'm going to talk about now because it was this 'Futurist' mentality that really struck with me more than anything else. It's also important that it also took two traumatic events to get to that point.

Further back I've mentioned two dates, late 2008 and early 2014. Late 2008 was for me what the Cave was for Tony and early 2014 was for me what the Wormhole was for Tony. In late 2008, something happened that completely destabilised my views and beliefs about the world in general and, to counteract this, I buried the feelings and emotions that followed deep inside. Tony built a suit of armour to counteract his traumatic event and in their own twisted way both actions worked to do something about the trauma. They were a form of protection. I buried any emotion and tried to live on having walled the emotion up behind whatever mental blocker I could. Tony protected himself with an Iron suit. Yeah, that'll sort it.

You can't bury trauma though and someday it will return again. Trauma must be faced if you are to move on from it.

In early 2014, another event happened that reinforced the trauma from before. The event of late 2008 was a blip surely? *It wouldn't manifest itself again,* I thought. I'll just carry on and believe in the world in the same way I always did and hope the emotional protection I put in place compensates for that. It didn't...

You see in late 2008, my parents split up. To me, my parents' marriage was as much an institution as the oldest in the world and even though up until that time I was aware of relationships splitting and things like divorce. I assumed it would never happen to them or even me simply because we were good people, which sounds kind of stupid but as a kid it's just how I saw it. And even after that, when the event had turned my views and beliefs on its head, I still believed it would never happen to me because I'd buried my emotions and was reticent to see the change head on. I was a good person, so surely it will never happen to me, right?

Then comes early 2014 and I decide that there is someone I'm quite fond of, so I ask them out. This was the first person I'd asked out since my parents split up (Yeah, go on, laugh it up) and I was rejected. You could almost hear my near subterranean level trauma say "Alright, time to go to work." Now rejection doesn't sound too traumatic but I was an inward person who struggled with this kind of thing anyway and the trauma had been lurking deep down. I took it hard, and spent months completely paralysed with a mixture of confusion, fear and other negative feelings.

It didn't matter if I was a good person, something like this was going to happen eventually. The trauma would return to rear its ugly head and I'd have to deal with it again because I hadn't done it properly or healthily the first time. Tony could build a suit to protect him from any threat on Earth but there were much bigger threats waiting for him. His invincibility was something that doesn't exist and the Wormhole had to show him that for a second time.

A rejection and a Wormhole. In comes the term 'Futurist'.

I've already gone over what Tony did when his trauma really took hold but not what I did.

After that rejection when I was forced to realise the idea that there was no such thing as relationship invincibility, I did whatever I could to stop it ever happening again. Much like Tony building suits and machines to protect the Earth, I realised I couldn't ignore the trauma but it didn't mean I couldn't prepare for it. I spent countless hours poring over websites and articles on how to maintain a proper and healthy relationship, how to communicate properly to your partner at any given time. I learnt how to do as many things around the house as I could, as many household jobs as possible. After all I didn't want to come across as lazy that might trigger the unspeakable. I've said already that I consider my writing to be a kind of obsession, albeit a good one. This was not the good kind of obsession.

Love and by extension relationships are something we can't really quantify because they involve so much emotion, which we also can't really quantify and yet that's what I tried to do. I tried to turn that side of life, something we can't predict or measure into a science, a formula. It wouldn't go wrong that way. Turns out that can be just as detrimental as trying to ignore your trauma because trying to prepare for every eventuality, especially in regard to the unpredictability of emotions is impossible and exhausting. You just end up losing yourself among other things.

But much like Tony, I really tried to do what I could to prepare and hopefully circumvent something I dreaded and feared. I even sabotaged what could have been a good friendship with the person by waiting a while and then asking them out again, just as a friend, but I'm sure they saw beyond that. I just plain refused to see it as it was and believed if I was 'better', then eventually it would work out.

Tony believed that if he continued to improve his armoured suits, then eventually nothing would be able to defeat him.

We were work colleagues and we continued to work together for another year before they left for another job. It was only after they left that I began to realise what I had done and how much the trauma had taken over. That left me in a worse place than before and yet in a way, I couldn't stop and kept on thinking that there must be something I was missing that was key. I had to keep working at it.

Long live The Futurists.

That's the problem with great Trauma, it not only destroys your sense of continuity but it also becomes your identity. I've mentioned it before but those thoughts consumed entire years for me, other things began to fade away as I marshalled everything I had on preventing the past from repeating itself. Tony may have confidently declared he was Iron Man but he was almost giving power to his own emotional and mental protection. Trauma becomes you.

But it's not all bad thankfully. Once you acknowledge that trauma inside you and take steps to face it, you can not only accept it but see it in a new light. I've mentioned how I went to therapy but I also looked at the manic preparation techniques I'd gone through in a new light afterwards. I'd exhausted myself but it doesn't mean I can't use what I'd learned. I stopped being so determined in learning every possible thing and appreciated the fact that I knew how better to communicate about all the various jobs and life skills I'd learned and used them to just help out rather than in some grand prevention of cataclysm.

Later on in Tony's journey he becomes a surrogate father to Peter Parker. Peter then represents everything Tony fears in a single person, a physical manifestation of what scares him. The two grow close and so Tony has to protect Peter much like he has worked to protect the entirety of Earth but as I'm sure everybody knows, Peter Parker is Spider-Man and he follows Tony into whatever danger is in front of him because he's also a superhero and that's what Tony would do. And eventually, circumstance would have it that Tony loses Peter. His worst fears come to pass and no amount of technology at his disposal could save Peter from death. All that work was for nought, Tony's attempts to prepare for everything to essentially destroy the trauma, doesn't work and he's left broken again.

Five years pass and Tony moves on and builds a real family, leaving the superhero life behind but eventually they come up with a plan to bring Peter and the other 50 percent of the universe back (So 50 percent of the universe essentially dies, I won't go into much detail because it's kind of complicated and I don't want to bore anyone with the details). More importantly, it's Tony who spearheads the idea that leads them to bringing everybody back, Peter included. That technology he'd become so reliant on does eventually end up saving everybody. I think it's important because even after Tony's worst fears had come to pass, he still used that same technology he'd worked to prevent that very event to save everyone. The technology was almost like a symptom of that original trauma that led to his rebirth in the Cave, it was a part of him forever and yet when acknowledged properly it can be just as much a benefit as a detriment.

Trauma becomes a part of your identity. It's too grand for it not too but it's important it doesn't dominate your identity. When Tony confidently said that he was Iron Man in the first film, it was a firm declaration of identity but it was a declaration of the protection he'd built for himself and how the trauma of that time in the Cave had taken hold of his identity. The moment in the wormhole only cemented that trauma and consumed Tony even more, making him work tirelessly to prevent that which had become him. Same with me, I gave myself protection in the form of ignorance after the first traumatic event and then become just as much of a 'Futurist' after the second.

I've come to accept the trauma that I have and have looked at everything I did in a new light. I still hope my trauma never comes to pass but with what I learned and taught myself in that time I can at least use that to temper my anxiety. All those new life skills may not prevent what may pass but at least I'll be well-prepared when I eventually, someday, move into a place of my own. I think that's what is important to remember about trauma, it can't be destroyed or be permanently rid of. It will just be there. Let it be a part of you, just not all of you.

Mine has made me more cautious, yes, but also a lot more knowledgeable about how relationships work, the good and bad. Tony took his and helped people, cared for people and eventually saved people. His Futurist ideals may not have prevented his worst fears but they still helped and afterwards he still uses that to save everybody that was lost.

And in the end, he faces the Mad Titan himself. The cause of that great cataclysm that led to 50 percent of life to die out and the physical manifestation of his fears and trauma. Between Tony and the others, they've saved everybody and it's up to Tony to use one last thing he's built to banish the Mad Titan and his trauma forever. This will, however, cost Tony his own life but everybody is safe and his long life's work will finally be done.

Before going out for good, he turns to the Mad Titan and speaks his final words. In that moment, he confidently says the only thing he could possibly say.

I am Iron Man.

Why do we Fall?

Go back and you'll note I've already touched on the character of Batman and how, even though I spent a lot of time in the past being a little obsessed with the character, he has since faded away when it comes to thinking about the fictional characters that have had any kind of great effect on me.

And yet when I was writing through that section, I remembered that the three Batman films directed by Christopher Nolan, commonly dubbed *The Dark Knight Trilogy*, remain my absolute favourite films of all time. They continue to provide the primary source of inspiration whenever I'm writing or planning any kind of story. No matter the genre, length or type, I always look to these three films, especially the final film *The Dark Knight Risers* for as much inspiration as possible. I can watch them over and over again without getting tired of them and generally consider them to be the best of the best, not just the pinnacle of their genre.

So with all this talk of relations to fictional characters and how Batman doesn't necessarily fit into that, why are these films so important to me when they're about, well,

Batman. Well, after really taking some time to think on it, it may not be the main character that has always drawn me but the story itself and the whole tapestry it weaves when the entire trilogy is done, start to finish, which, in a way, is kind of the point of these films. That it's about more than just one man, about a symbol and what that symbol represents, so that's kind of meta I suppose.

This isn't to say Batman isn't awesome because to me he's never looked better than in these films. The bike chase from the third film is pure cinema and the scene later on in the film when Bruce climbs out of the pit is my favourite scene from any film. But when you watch the whole trilogy and consider what happens to Bruce in the context of these films, you realise that these films aren't necessarily about Batman in the way that you would assume they are.

The question at the top of this section is prevalent in all three films and is notably never spoken to 'Batman' but always to Bruce Wayne because when it's all said and done, it's his story. And yes, in the end, the question is answered.

Batman is immortal, right? I mean as a cultural icon. Characters come and go from the collective consciousness but very few have the cultural standing as Batman. He's been around for many years before I was even born and I'm sure he'll still be around as a cultural titan even after I've passed on. Millions look up to him and some even want to be him, which I think has to do with the fact that he's just a regular human underneath that suit. No radioactive spider bite or power of flight, just a normal man who puts on some bat inspired protective gear and fights crime. He can't use super strength or super speed to stop criminals, he has to use his wits and strategic mind to outsmart them. I guess that's what makes him so likeable and imitable, anybody could do it in a way, well, apart from being a billionaire but I suppose even that's not entirely impossible.

And there's the tragic origins of Bruce's journey to becoming that fabled hero. It's not much of a spoiler, I'm sure everybody knows that Bruce's parents get shot in an alley after a night at the opera. God only knows it's been in every single Batman film. That tragic night though is the catalyst to Bruce becoming Batman without the death of his parents to a mugger, Gotham would never have its caped crusader to defend them.

Throughout the many incarnations of Batman we've had, that fact never changes. Bruce Wayne will always be there to witness his parents die in that alley and that will birth Batman or the idea of Batman at the very least. It defines Bruce Wayne and every action he takes from that point onwards. And in the age-old comic books and films preceding, Batman would live on fighting crime forever because of this. Batman was Bruce Wayne's fate.

What's interesting about *The Dark Knight Trilogy* though is that it was made with the determination for it to have a defining beginning and end. The beginning was the same, parents die, trains with shadowy cabal of ninjas but they had to figure out how the story was going to end. Like I said, in the comics, Batman was forever but in film everybody ages and rather than go the James Bond route where the actor essentially swaps out for a younger version every few films, they wanted this to be self-contained. For the first time, the superhero would not be 'Forever'.

So surely the inevitable conclusion is that Batman perishes? He does but Bruce Wayne doesn't and whether you buy into the fact that this trilogy was either planned or not planned from the start, this suits the character of Batman almost better than any other hero. Why? Because his parents got shot.

Superman descended from the heavens (Well, another planet), Spider-man was bitten by a radioactive spider, other heroes are literally born as gods but Bruce watched his parents get shot by a mugger. I'm sure a lot of people want to be Batman because he's the most probable hero to be, he's just human after all. But I'm sure most people don't want to watch their parents get shot and killed. It's a deeply tragic and yet deeply human and relatable origin for a hero and the sole reason Bruce fights the criminal underworld every night.

It's the tragedy that must prevail to give the world one of its greatest modern hero's and yet it's Bruce's tragedy. That's what these films focus on. The idea of Batman in these films isn't that Batman is Bruce Wayne's final form, it's that Batman is the final phase for Bruce Wayne in his decade spanning journey to move on and to leave the world he thought he knew behind a little better than that night he lost his parents.

I've already mentioned when talking about Tony Stark that most superhero films use the idea of the real identity of the hero struggling to contain their heroic identity a secret as an easy source of conflict because the ultimate goal is to have the two sides combine, unite and coalesce to be immortal, battling forever. They want the human side of the person to cross with the super heroic so that they can balance both sides of life forever for the greater good and all that. But these films want you to see Batman and Bruce Wayne as two very separate entities that the idea of Bruce Wayne being Batman forever is an act of pure self-destruction, almost akin to suicide. Batman doesn't get stronger over the course of these films, not like other heroes, he's only human after all. He takes arguably harder beatings, physically and emotionally, further on in his journey than at the beginning. He continues to take those beatings; he continues to fall. Why does he keep falling?

Why do we fall?

The answer according to the movie is 'So that we can learn to pick ourselves up'. It's a logical answer that can be taken very easily in the most literal sense. Suffered a failure? Taken a beating? Physical or emotionally, it pertains to the literal idea that all you have to do is brush it off and pick yourself up, I suppose it's similar to 'Practice makes Perfect' or to get better at something you just have to 'Try and try again'.

But like real life and even in the context of the films themselves, the answer isn't so simple and Bruce must learn that over the course of the story to truly move on. Not just from his mistakes but from his emotional trauma and the tragedy that dogs him every time he dons the suit. Most super-hero films would go for the literal approach and have the question be asked after the hero suffers a crushing defeat by the antagonist they're facing. The question and the subsequent answer would be the surge the hero needs to fight back and win the day. And, yeah, in *The Dark Knight Rises*, it's given to Bruce just before he climbs out of the pit, just before he returns to Gotham to wear the cape and cowl one last time.

And that's the key difference, the question isn't given to Batman. It's given to Bruce because Bruce knows that to continue on and to freely live, he must be rid of the Batman. And the final act of the Batman is for Bruce to let him be destroyed so that he can become the true symbol he was designed to be. Bruce gets to fulfil Alfred's wish of leading a normal life, one where he can find happiness away from the city that he felt compelled to change, to make better because he has his experiences, the death of his parents, compelled him to believe in the idea that something like that should never happen again and this led him to almost give his life to the city he wanted to change.

Finality for Bruce wasn't 'The Batman' but it was still a part of his identity. It was his beliefs, his experiences and fears all crafted into a force that would eventually outlive him for the greater good of protecting and safeguarding people. And maybe that's the final and purest destination of a person's identity, of their self. When it reaches a point where your ideals and belief have gained a life of their own and you can pass on, knowing with content that you've essentially lived beyond what your physical body can give and have become, well, a symbol.

I think that's what resonates with me most with these films. The idea that when you find your purpose and believe in it, knowing that there is good behind it that your ideals and beliefs can become more than just you and the one person. It applies to so many things that I've gone over already. Especially in writing and storytelling, I've gone over lots of reasons why I want to write and why I chose to write but this sense of the beyond is another. Christopher Nolan directed and co-wrote these films and when he eventually passes on, these films will still be around for people to enjoy and to inspire people who want to follow a similar path. Even after they were just released, they did this, no longer where they an idea in the mind of the Nolan brothers but they gained a life of their own and became something else for millions of people.

When I was going through many a rough period, the details of which I've already talked about, I would watch these films. It was the ultimate form of escapism for me and the times when Bruce, not Batman, would pick himself up after falling were inspiring to me as it gave me hope that we can all pick ourselves up from tragedy, trauma and pain. If I (hopefully) reach my goal of becoming a scriptwriter someday, it's something I hope, I can replicate in my own stories. It's not just about the enjoyment of writing for me but the idea that one day, a kid similar in age to me will watch a film I've had a hand in creating and be at least inspired to do more and to live on.

It's incredibly meta, these films that tell the story of a man creating a symbol that will live beyond him and give hope to people who suffer similar tragedies to himself gain a new kind of life. The films themselves become a symbol of hope for those that need it, much like the idea of 'The Batman' does for the people of Gotham. I've thought about what it would be like if I actually succeeded in my goals and aspirations. It would create this incredibly layered full circle moment. The films which inspired me, which I owe so much to and gave me something to look up to end up doing the same for someone else when I create my own and maybe that then inspires that person to do the same. And maybe that story of a man creating a Bat like symbol for his beliefs and for his city will be the story that resonates across those generations, just as it was designed to.

I've said that because of my nature I often look for greater meaning in what I do, whether it's work or any other aspect of life. These films and the ideas they convey are almost the closest example I can give to describing it properly. What better meaning for what you end up doing than for it outlive you and take on its own life. I thought that the idea of 'Work' was that you gave part of yourself up to provide for society in whatever way you deem best. I can personally think of no better way for my work to provide than for it to outlive me.

These films take the question of 'Could you be Batman'? and technically answer yes. Most of the time you'd quickly shut down the idea of being any superhero, even one as human as Batman because that kind of altruism is impossible for any one person to take on without completely destroying themselves. In the context of these particular films, it's Bruce Wayne who you couldn't be, not 'The Batman'. These films know that Bruce can't be Batman forever, they look at the idea of a Superhero in a realistic light and so the idea isn't that the two identities become one like in most superhero films and even in the comics. The idea that Bruce has is that when a criminal robs somebody and sees a bat like figure looming over them, it doesn't matter who is under the cowl, they'd run in fear because it's the image and the symbolism of Batman that scares them.

Bruce takes the trauma of his childhood and not only eventually owns it but projects that ownership back to such a degree that it outlives him. That part of his identity, the will to fight back against that which destroyed him emotionally and mentally goes on to live beyond him for others to pick up.

I've mentioned this already but it bears repeating that trauma is something to be owned and accepted. It can't be destroyed or be made to disappear and so whether you accept it or not, it becomes a part of your identity and the formation of your identity. Trauma will shape everything from memory to experience, to beliefs and so anybody that goes through it must learn to find a positive way to move on in life while still knowing it's there. Knowing that wherever you go and whatever you do, it will have its say. You are your trauma in a way.

I've been through my own sense of trauma and went for years thinking that if I buried it and ignored, it then it would go away but it was only after I went through that yearlong healing process that I learnt to accept it as being a part of me and let it inform me but not control me.

I saw that in a character I admire and respect, Tony Stark. watching his journey showed me that a person can take something like that and use it for something better to eventually save more than himself and to heal his wounds, even if it takes a while to get there. He accepted who he was and was proud of it – his declaration of his identity, good and bad, showed that in the end.

And finally, there's Bruce Wayne, who takes that idea to such a level that it becomes more than the man that is Bruce Wayne. His identity moulded by the tragedy of his parent's death and the trauma of his experiences in the cave full of bats transcend him and becomes not just his fight but the fight of others long after him.

That's why I find these films to be my absolute favourite and, in the end, why the character of Batman doesn't necessarily mean as much to me because it was never about the character of Batman but the idea of Batman. When a person goes through trauma, great or not, it can often mean it becomes synonymous with their identity and their core self. It can become hard to imagine the same idea of a future you once had because something terrible has begun to shape it.

But only if you let it.

The question of *'Why do we Fall'?* that's often asked in these films is always answered with *'So we can learn to pick ourselves up'*. When we allow trauma to control us, to shape us at its will, we fall. When we acknowledge it and accept it, we pick ourselves up and learn from that mistake. It will always be there to inform your actions and decisions but you can use that in a positive way.

Maybe that is how you're truly conquer trauma and become your best self, your purest identity. Not just by accepting and growing with it like I did and then using it for the greater good like Tony did but by doing what Bruce did and making sure that that acceptance and idealism lives on after you. Which is why in the context of *The Dark Knight Trilogy*, anyone can be 'Batman' because 'Batman' isn't just the immortal character who's been around for years, it's an idea that can be used by anyone.

It's of one boy's hope that not only can he accept the trauma he gained on that terrible night…

But that we all can.

Chapter Five
Obstacles

Stupid obstacles. So, I've gone over trauma, which is an obstacle in itself but there are also other obstacles. Sometimes they're not the kind you can predict and sometimes they're made by other people, albeit with good-natured intentions. But safe to say, they can sometimes be something that challenges us. Challenge is good, however, and it can lead to us growing in interesting directions but, anyway, onto the stupid obstacles.

The Needs of the many outweigh the needs of the few
However…
The Ends do not Justify the Means…

People keep telling me I should go on holiday. No, not just take a holiday (I'm at the tail-end of a holiday right now). I get a good six or seven weeks away from work every year, which unfortunately seem to be going faster and faster each time. Especially this one, which has felt like it's over before it's even started.

But, for now, that's beside the point. Like I said, people seem to think I should go on holiday like away on holiday, you know, to some far-off land. I'm not so sure if I should or should I say if I want to.

Because you have to want to, right? You have to actually want to go away somewhere. That's the point of a holiday, isn't it? To want to visit a different country so that you can relax or sight see, right now, I don't necessarily need to go away. I mean sure I want to visit places like America and Japan someday but right now I don't feel like I need it.

And that got me thinking. It has been playing on my mind, do people think I need a holiday or that I should be going on holiday? And this line of thinking, then led down another rabbit-hole of thinking about what I thought I wanted and needed and what I do now.

I hear it at work all the time, "I really need a holiday" or "God, I need to go away". You need to? I mean, yeah, cool, if that's what you really need and that's what will keep you from losing your damn mind, then go for it. I always thought that missed the point of going away though.

I thought you went somewhere new to enjoy it because you wanted it. Saying you need to go away just makes it sound like you're trying to escape from the regularity of the day to day (I'm sorry if this comes across as bad, please, refer to very top). That's when the whole thing about your own day to day rears its head again (Yep, we're circling back to the beginning again).

Escapism as a want is fun but escapism as a need is dangerous.

When I was younger, I thought I had an idea of what I wanted and needed, the terms didn't have any differentiation for me. After all, when I was growing up my family would go on about how I needed a job, a house, a girl a regular place to go out to...you know the rest. And I absolutely drilled that into my head because that's probably the same advice everybody else my age was getting. And why not? It's perfectly sound advice for someone who was reserved and didn't seem like he had any idea of the world and its workings.

So then why the ominous wording, you ask? Well, for all its good intentions and let me make absolutely clear I'm sure this advice was given with care and good intentions in mind, it doesn't seem like that's what's in store for me. I'm still kind of coming to terms with this...

Before I went to therapy for my wonderful menagerie of mental health issues (Including but not limited to moderate depression and severe anxiety), I was almost in a constant marathon with my own self to meet the targets that I thought were there and set to lead to the ideal life (I know this advice was given with good intentions, so I apologise if this comes across as slightly antagonistic or ungrateful). However, hard I tried though, there was always this sense of detachment from those attempts like something didn't feel quite right.

It was only after therapy that I realised that I didn't really align with those ideals, not yet anyway. It was tough to come to that realisation especially when those ideals aren't necessarily tailored to me personally but are ideals that pretty much everybody had been brought up with. Whether everybody followed them, I don't know but in failing to meet them myself it may have been another catalyst for my issues. It's only after going through therapy and learning to appreciate my individuality that I realised that, for now, I'm maybe on a different path.

If this was a Venn diagram, it would probably cross over a lot with my traits as an introvert and this is where the difference between wants and needs come in for me.

Take the idea of a relationship, a girlfriend. Do I want one? Someday, yeah, I'll probably find someone I want to enter a relationship with but as of now I don't need one. Pre-therapy me would say different that person would be riddled with anxiety about how they're somehow behind everybody else. Now, I'm more than happy and accepting spending time by myself until the right time and the right person.

While before I was anxious to keep up in the race of life with everybody else to get it all right and get it all done, now it just feels like a checklist I was desperate to complete and after getting to understand myself better that's not really how I want these things. I'm more than happy to wait for the right time. Right now, there are other things I'd like to concentrate on.

It's interesting watching some people I remember from school getting all these things without a second thought, after all, that's how it should be, right?

But before this comes off like a dig at those I used to know and, in some cases, still know, some of them are very happy and satisfied with the direction their life has gone and that's great. It's just that after spending most of my life feeling like I was behind everybody else it's nice to have come to an inner realisation that it's OK in wanting and needing different things.

Also, may I once again repeat that I love all my family and I'm sure their advice was well founded and is much appreciated but you know what life is like with its Curveballs. It just so happens the Curveball is writing this.

Ugh, after all, that maybe I should go on holiday.

I have always wanted to visit Japan...

Or go back to Disneyland (I'm deadly serious)

Routine does not allow us to progress – unknown...

If there's one job that fiction and media like to portray as being the death knell of the soul, it's the desk job.

The dreaded desk job in the plain office with the perfectly angular desk as well as the tens of other identical cubicles that surround the very one I'm describing right now. It's the banner flag of administration and bureaucracy. The language of the office is often purely corporate to a totalitarian point. Consumer! Buzzwords! The Bottom Line!

But that's not entirely fair to the desk job. I guess it's just the easiest target to hit because there are a whole host of other jobs that can encompass this feeling for an individual and even then, it might just be the mix of the job and the individual that creates this feeling of silent and subtle imprisonment. The overall message is the same though that sense that you're working on autopilot and that same dire routine everyday has almost caused time to halt. Well, until you're too old to carry on, then I guess you're just swapped out for a more efficient model.

Sorry, came close to ranting a bit there.

But as I've mentioned before, there are positive arguments to be made. After all, it's a job, a place of employment! The folks at the head of the board are paying you and there's a provided place to eat and chat with everybody else who suspiciously all have baggy eyes and a drained aura but, hey, you're safe, right? This boring, glum job with the even more boring and plain décor and the almost identical looking workforce is a place of safety and a feeling of safety is a feeling of contentment but when did contentment and safety equate to happiness? Because when you're stuck chasing safety and contentment rather than happiness, which even I'll admit can be tricky to categorise for an individual, then you risk something far more dangerous than you realise. It's a danger that's difficult to see and isn't as tangible as an illness or a physical danger that you can reach out and touch. Most of all though, it can creep in and cripple every aspect of your life without you even realising what's happening. Allow me to explain…

So far, various sections you've read have focused on one particular fictional character. This one will focus on two, not only to shake things up a bit but the contrast helps cement my point I suppose. That, and not only is this about me personally but it's kind of about everybody and how that generic office job portrayal isn't something to be so easily dismissed. It may not comprise the most important message in fiction but there's a message there, none the less, and it does tie in with the bigger picture.

Exhibit A is Nathan Drake.

Nathan Drake is the star of the critically acclaimed and downright awesome *Uncharted* series of games. Even people who don't have much of a knowledge of video games might have heard of *Uncharted*. For those who haven't or just aren't sure what *Uncharted* is or who Nathan Drake is, the games are basically the *Indiana Jones* of video games. Adventure, treasure hunting and that dabble in the weird and supernatural make up the core DNA of both these franchises. And for the first three games in the franchise, the *Uncharted* series pretty much followed the *Indiana Jones* formula as much as it could within the differing confines of a video game. It's the fourth game, though, that does things a little differently.

It's no secret that not a lot of people are fond of the fourth *Indiana Jones* film, I actually don't mind it too much but the fourth *Uncharted* game and the fourth Indiana Jones film take a similar concept but apply it in radically different ways. They both deal with ageing protagonists, however, *Indiana Jones* remains the same pulp adventure it was in the previous films. His old age is more or less played for laughs than it is a serious discussion on how that kind of life, which is dangerous, can start to take its toll in the person, whether it's directly or indirectly, such as their outside circle of close ones.

Nathan Drake isn't as old as Indy when we return to him in *Uncharted 4* but he's already retired from his adventuring lifestyle and has settled down with his wife, Elena and taken a job with a Marine Hauling company. He even jokes at one point that his daily treasure finds now consist of semi-trucks rather than priceless and ancient treasure. He's sworn off that old life and is dedicated to living a normal life with Elena. He's quit cold turkey.

Well, *Uncharted 4* wouldn't be a very satisfying game if Nathan didn't return to his adventuring lifestyle during the runtime and due to an incident with his long lost, thought to be dead brother, he's quickly back at it. Nathan and his brother globetrotting and dodging angry mercenaries while they look for a lost pirate's treasure. They need to find it to pay off a nasty individual who Nathan's brother supposedly owes and Nathan uses this excuse to justify him putting himself back in danger. He even believes this for a lot of the game's story.

But when Elena catches up to him in *Madagascar* after he'd spent weeks lying to her, she sees right through the excuse. Nathan isn't just doing this for his brother. Big part of him misses the lifestyle of adventure and danger. The lure of treasure and the next great find. The experience is a learning curve for both of them while on a remote island, looking for the lost pirate colony of Libertalia, Elena saves Nathan from a near death experience and over the course of the rest of the game, they both come to accept the fact that this life really is the one meant for them.

Elena even says towards the final moments of the game, "I think in our attempt to lead a normal life, we may have overshot."

The idea that these two could spend years of their life experiencing life changing moments in places like the Himalayas, the Middle-East and South America, only to then try and settle down to the notion of a normal life becomes a little ludicrous. Their lives beforehand were fraught with danger, including consistent gunfights with disgruntled thugs of all shapes and sizes but it matched their skill and their knowledge. They were also passionate about it, able to push on through incredible circumstances through sheer will. There could be no true normal life for these two because that picture like ideal couldn't fulfil them in the end.

As the game ends, they use the treasure they found in Libertalia to buy the hauling company and travel the world looking for rare underwater finds. There'd be no gunfights and close escapes but they'd be using their knowledge, skill and love for the next great find to satisfy themselves and create their normal life, not the normal life. The player leaves Nathan Drake behind, knowing that while he won't be adventuring any longer, he'll at least finally be happy.

Exhibit B. Robert Parr or should I say Mr Incredible.

Surely, everybody knows what *The Incredibles* is right.

That ridiculously good *Pixar* film about the family of superheroes made in 2004. A film that is as much about the family dynamic and structure as it is about superhero action. If you've seen the film and you most definitely should have by now, then you'll remember at the start of the film, Mr Incredible is a well-known superhero in his prime. He's about to get married to Elastigirl, Helen Parr but decides he's got time to stop a few crimes before he gets hitched.

One crime he stops or thinks he stops is a man falling from a high floor of a skyscraper. Turns out the guy didn't want to be saved if you catch my drift and so Mr Incredible and by all accounts every superhero is sued by the government and along with his fellow supers is forced to renounce his identity and go into hiding.

The mighty Mr Incredible is now just regular Robert Parr and regular Robert Parr now works in literally the exact same type of office desk job I was describing at the start of this section. Everything is there, the angular desk, the plain décor, the tens of absolutely identical cubicles. He now works in the insurance sector and it is not treating him well. He's out of shape, has hilariously droopy eyes and just generally looks like he's lost any passion for, well, anything in life. Bob is secretly desperate to return to his old life as Mr Incredible, his den at his house shows this in great detail but he can't. Heroics are gone, outlawed and for the sake of his family, he has to be satisfied with the office.

Well, thank God someone wants to kill off all the superheroes.

A woman named Mirage working under the orders of a mysterious benefactor (It's the villain, duh), offers Bob the chance to become Mr Incredible again. Yeah, there's a malfunctioning killer robot but there can be a Mr Incredible again. Bob can return to the glory days. He has to keep it a secret though, he's certain no one would understand his need to be Mr Incredible again. Not after everyone has seemingly come to accept their new lives of relative normalcy.

So Mr Incredible jets off to Nomanisan Island (Read it carefully...) time and time again, fighting killer robot after killer robot. Helen and the rest of his family believe what Bob has told them that he's earned a gushing promotion at the office and he's flying away for conference meetings, not that he was fired for launching his boss through about six walls. For a while they suspect nothing, however, Bob is in better shape, a better mood and is building a much better relationship with everyone in his family. He isn't at the boring office though instead he's jetting off to a hidden island with no help and only killer robots for company. Bob has gone from the safest place on the planet to quite possibly the most dangerous.

And yet he's the happiest he's ever been.

After Bob is beaten by a version of the robot too powerful even for him and captured by the villain, Syndrome, his family soon finds out exactly what he's been doing for these past months. Helen obviously isn't happy that Bob has been lying to her while their kids are just happy with the new super suits given to them. They eventually rescue Bob and spend the rest of the movie working together, trying to stop Syndrome from enacting his terrible plan.

Bob is scolded and reprimanded by Helen for lying to her and for his actions but he isn't forced to give up his super-hero ways. Instead, as a family, they work through it and find a way to acknowledge that Bob, and by extension all of them, would be better off being Superheroes regardless of the consequences. So are born *The Incredibles*.

That's what I love about both similar stories. Two people who try and accept the normal life or the standard picture of it and discover that while it's certainly safer to make a living at the desk, their past experiences and natural skills mean that, eventually, they'll need to return to what they do best for the sake of themselves and those around them.

I'll admit that they definitely go about it the wrong way. Both end up lying to their significant others to indulge their passions in the name of 'Protecting their loved ones' and both are discovered and severely punished for it (I only just noticed how similar these two stories are, remote jungle island, villain who has a history with the hero, both heroes succeed by accepting a group dynamic, weird...) but while you, as an audience member, are shown that they made bad choices in doing what they wanted, eventually, you and the story itself accept that these two are being who they are meant to be and in both instances, the hero's respective loved ones, learn that these two are in fact much happier, healthier and even more loving personalities when they do what they're really good at.

Because sometimes the danger is worth it. I don't know if it's just me but lately there seems to be a blurring of the lines when it comes to safety and happiness. Some people are content and acceptant to stay where they are, even an inch out of the comfort zone proving too scary of a task. But maybe a dose of danger can be good for us, for our sense of wellbeing. I'm not talking about the kind of danger that Nathan Drake or Mr Incredible pursue. I'm pretty sure none of us have to worry about killer robots but when you get that feeling, that hint that you can do better, that something else is out there for you, maybe it's worth it.

Now I'm not advocating everybody walk into their boring jobs tomorrow and throw in the towel because I'd rather not see infrastructures topple and there's a time and place for crazy impulsive decisions. The point of these two stories is that Nathan and Bob mess up a lot more than they could of by impulsively throwing themselves back into danger and while risking a little financial or emotional danger might be necessary in finding your true north in life. There's a better way to do whatever it is you need to do. As I've mentioned before, I want to be a professional writer but even I haven't left my job because I've come to learn it would probably be a bad idea to just walk out with nothing but lofty dreams and optimism (Although they can be all you need to get going) but it's that idea that safety is enough. I could get all political and economic and launch into a tirade I've heard numerous times about how there aren't as many jobs around anymore and we should be lucky to be earning but I'm sure we've all had enough of that argument. There's truth to it, for sure, but what good did it ever do anyone to anchor themselves at whatever job they landed at and stick with it because it was safe.

If these two stories have taught me anything, it's that while there is certainly a wrong way to do it, Nathan Drake and Mr Incredible had good intentions at heart because forcing themselves to try and live the normal life, as safe as possible, would never satisfy them. These were two people with skill, talent and a lust for what they did and when really let free to do this became the best versions of themselves. For them, safety wasn't happiness. They needed danger in a way. They just needed to remember and work with the people around them, especially their loved ones to make sure they could be the happiest they could be.

The office job or variant of it might be the true north for some people. The safety might be enough for them but for those who have had that moment where they suddenly remember that outlandish dream they never got around to following or that untapped skill they wanted to refine, just remember that as long as you think it through and involve those around you, sometimes a little danger might be just what you need.

Elena – I think in our attempt to lead a normal life, we may have overshot.

Nathan – Y'know…it won't be easy.

Elena – Nothing worthwhile ever is…

When you gaze long into an abyss, the abyss gazes also into you – Friedrich Nietzsche

There is a universal fear shared by the entirety of the human race. It's such a universal fear because there is no way to beat it and accepting it seems to be almost impossible, as the fact that it has the ultimate finality about it means that we cannot see beyond it.

I can't think of anyone that doesn't fear death.

Maybe a fair few have accepted the notion that they are mortal and will eventually pass on to the great beyond but even in their final moments, there will almost certainly be a sense of anxiousness and fear. After all, who knows what is behind that final curtain when we pass on and find ourselves away from the world as we know it, what is on the other side?

There are countless theories, beliefs and supposed answers as to what lies on the other side. An afterlife, reincarnation, some people believe there is nothing…just eternal darkness. With so many theories and no concrete answers, it's relatively easy to imagine why anybody and everybody would be frightened of passing on of leaving everything they know and have experienced behind.

But I've always found the fear of death to be an odd fear, especially when you look at every other fear in the world. If someone is scared of a grisly death, then fair play because I'm sure every one of us would prefer to pass on peacefully but the idea of being scared of dying is strange to me because like anything else in life, it can almost come down to what might happen, the unknown. What if you find out that in the future you die peacefully and on the other side, there really is a beautiful paradise waiting, afterlife as a utopia. What's so bad about that?

I know nobody knows what is on the other side and unfortunately some people are going to die uncomfortable deaths. It's a shame but it's true but if the case were that there is a golden afterlife, what is to fear?

It's the unknown that is to fear. Maybe the universal fear we all share isn't death but the fear of the unknown.

Going into anything in life without any prior knowledge or idea of what could be waiting for you is a stressful and scary thought. It doesn't matter what the circumstance is, people prefer going into anything with some idea, some notion of what is going to happen and what to expect. That way, they can prepare accordingly and steel themselves with whatever they can find in the hopes that they can prevail if needs be. The more a person knows and has, the safer they will feel. When something is truly unknown, no amount of positive thinking can circumvent that feeling of dread and loneliness that takes hold. The unknown then can be perceived as overwhelmingly negative.

But the unknown isn't a benevolent or malevolent force that decides how to treat each individual – it's just what we don't know and while that can be scary, sometimes stepping into the unknown can turn into triumph as much as it can turn into disaster. The unknown is just chance, randomness, only it can appear to be on a much grander scale, depending on the circumstance surrounding the individual. The pull of the unknown is our best chance at growth a lot of the time, regardless of the outcome, the moments when we step out into what we don't know can change us for the better.

But to do that, you must confront the fear. You know what they say about fear though, the only thing to fear is fear itself and when fear becomes the stronger force, that can lead to complacency, stagnation and overwhelming dread. It's one of the hardest things to overcome fear but when a person does, there are very few things more cathartic.

The fear of the unknown is one I still struggle with. I'm a lot more aware and knowledgeable of it than I once was but I still find myself hesitating to do things sometimes.

There's always that creeping notion in my head that something will go wrong that maybe something won't be as I expect in a horrifying way. I've told you already that I want to be a professional writer, specifically a scriptwriter and that for me, it represents the ultimate goal. It's everything I could ever want and it's something I've wanted for over ten years now. It's taken me a long time to get over a series of fears regarding this ambition though.

When I first began to write to try and flex my skills, I struggled with the idea of being good enough to do it. I could have all the passion and drive in the world but how would I know if I was going to be skilled enough to make this my profession and career. It hampered my focus and led me to procrastinate a lot. The thing with writing is it's obviously linked to creativity and creativity is like a muscle, you have to practice and work at it to improve. If you're scared of your lack of ability, how can you improve it?

It took a while but eventually I got over the idea of not being good enough. It's not that I didn't care. I always looked to improve and write the best I could but I let go of the idea of it being absolutely perfect in every aspect. I'd always aim to write a great piece but I wouldn't sweat the small details if I couldn't solve them. I'd just keep writing. Eventually I did notice I was improving. I'd go back and look at old stories and I'd be able to spot mistakes and other things that weren't working. I also knew what to do to remedy the fault – the more I noticed this, the more I felt confident in my abilities. The fear faded and I just kept writing, planning and working away.

There is another fear though – one which will be harder to confront. It's kind of a Catch 22. This one hasn't been around for as long as the other. It's only made itself known since I've found my confidence and self-belief in my writing and it links right back to that fear of the unknown and the other side.

What if I make it and it's not what I thought? What if it turns out to be a horrible nightmare?

A far more crippling fear than the other, this one can't easily be fixed by daily practice or a positive mind-set. This requires me to actually succeed at what I want to do. I think that's what makes it more powerful than the other. There's no turning back with this one as I'll have already made it. Every time I sit down and write or plan or just study a technique, this fear rears its head. I've put countless hours and effort into following this ambition and my instinct says to keep going but there is that constant voice somewhere inside that keeps telling me how it might turn out. It takes some work trying to shut it out every time I sit down to write.

There is one small consolation to this dilemma though and it relates to the place I work and a part of it I used to work at. See, everywhere has its messages and lessons. You see, for about five years, I worked at the filling station. For a little while I was fine with it, as anybody would be but as a lot of people can relate to, after a couple of years, boredom and restlessness started to set in. I was starting to become desperate to leave the station and as I've often said, I wanted to follow my ambitions. When I'd had a particularly bad day or possibly bad week, I sheepishly wandered into the personnel office and made my intention known that I was leaving. You know, just going.

I understand now that that would've been a stupid idea.

Suggestions were made that I either move department, which at the time I had no interest in or find a completely new place of employment. The idea was I needed an income and so just leaving wouldn't have been the smartest move in the world. Neither idea interested me, I thought that the filling station was the best department at the company for me. I'd spent so long on there that the idea of learning a new set of departmental skills felt like unnecessary slow down. I could phase through a day at the station, leaving my mind fresh for any writing. Even though I barely wrote at the time.

Finding another place of employment was the same problem, only accentuated to a far greater level. At least with the first problem I'd still be at the same company. Not only that but my current employers were understanding with what hours I wanted to work and why.

So, I reduced my weekly hours and just continued with working at the filling station, even though it felt draining and I didn't have any drive to work on anything else. I'd learned to phase through my day at petrol, leaving my mind dormant in the hopes it wouldn't be tired for any creative work. It was only a couple of years later when I was suddenly moved away from the filling station that I realised my unfounded fears from moving where damaging my drive and focus.

The one department I'd completely shunned and had absolutely no intention of working on were the checkouts, the tills. Me sat on a checkout, serving a growing line of people until my hours were done didn't sound appealing, even though in hindsight, it was essentially the same as the filling station, just with more food.

Guess where I was moved to…

I can't remember why I was moved. I think there may have been a store wide shuffle or something but I was moved onto the checkouts, apparently temporarily but I didn't think that was true. I was all but certain, I wasn't going back. After spending a couple of years feeling lethargic and miserable at the filling station, I was confronted with the fears I'd created for myself. I had to adapt but, by some stroke of fate, it was exactly what I needed.

I was only on the checkouts for about a month before I got a permanent position on the stores stock control team, which was a far cry from the filling station and required me to have to learn an entirely new skillset and completely readjust what I'd got suited to. As it turns out, once I'd spent a few weeks getting used to the new placement, I didn't feel slowed down by the change. I was almost reinvigorated. It might have something to do with the fact that my time in therapy was during this transition but ever since joining the new department, I've written more than I ever did in the years before it.

Yes, I still want to leave and pursue my ambitions but ever since the change I've felt my mind come back to life, the drive that had disappeared was back. This new department required my full attention and focus to do the job right. It was something I'd feared, how can I concentrate on a different career path if I'm focused on doing another job, right? When I was at the station, I believed in resting my mind as much as possible to keep it fresh. All that did was shut my mind down, while now, because I was forced to focus and work my brain properly, it started to reinvigorate my brain in all areas.

My fear was unfounded because I'd gotten used to a certain way of thinking. I'd gotten lazy and was thinking with tunnel vision.

After I'd started to get back to working well again in both areas, writing and my actual current job, I had a thought. My original fear was unfounded by beginning to learn again and focus permanently, I began to write and enjoy writing again. So, if change had made me better and get me closer to my goals, what other fears would I be wrong about?

Maybe all these intricate fears and anxieties about what it might be like if I eventually made it would also be nothing but illusions and I'd very much enjoy and belong in the place I always thought I did. What if I just trusted that deep inner compass and followed it rather than spending time thinking about tiny details that probably wouldn't matter in the long run? Big changes might still be scary and uncomfortable but a small change at work made me realise that maybe it wasn't impossible for me to adjust and adapt. I wonder (and maybe hope) if that is the last fear, the last roadblock I must face before I, hopefully, make it to the end.

But apart from that lethargy and sense of laziness I'd adopted, there was a fear of moving away from the familiar. For a multitude of reasons, I stoically believed that staying exactly where I was would end up being the best course of action for my long-term goals, there really was nothing to fear but fear itself and maybe it was fear that was causing my mind to create all of these small, insignificant reasons for stopping still. I was scared of the unknown, the other side and that was a fear I couldn't afford to adopt because it's the other side that is the destination I want to reach. I just need to trust that the other side is a better place than my expectations have set it up to be.

Being such an insular and creative person meant that these large variety of fears, big and small, were very easy to create as well. It was probably another reason why I suffer so easily from anxiety and why it's categorised as severe in my case. I tried to use a kind of negative reinforcement to push me towards something better without realising that the negative reinforcement of habitual lethargy was enabling my anxiety to feed of the imaginative fears I'd created for not edging in any kind of direction.

The quote at the top of this section is a quote I love. I've always been fascinated in it since I read into its meaning and I like to think it connects to that idea of remembering your past and your history in case you happen to repeat mistakes. It's this idea that the 'abyss' in question is a force which the person is trying to defeat or overcome and in diverting all of their energy into fighting it, they become the 'abyss'. It's the hunter going out to fight monsters, only to return a monster himself.

The abyss or the monster can be described as fear as well. If you spend all of yourself fighting your fear, you may end up becoming your fear in a sense.

I have always wanted to leave my regular job behind and follow my passions but for a long time, I spent time and energy trying to limit my time and energy in various fractions of life so that I could spend real time writing. I ended up getting so obsessed with saving my energy everywhere I could that I just stopped trying in every way. I got scared that if I sacrificed some of that time and energy into maybe trying something different, it would derail everything. Even small, short-term changes were off putting to me.

It's only when I was forced to face that set of fears that I realised the trap I had set for myself. I was looking with tunnel vision and failed to notice that my insistence on saving myself and my energy had gone a bit too far. I think there's another saying about this, something about not seeing the woods for the trees.

It's strange thinking about where that thought train came from and especially how it affected me when I really lost sight of it. I've written more in this past year than any year, I've learnt a whole host of other things as well since that period of time where I was forced to change my position at work and not to forget the therapy I went through at the time. I don't think I would have gotten any much further with my work if I'd stopped where I was, still fearing the other side. I'm not as anxious about changes anymore. I know that if I have a strong anchor on myself and what I want and am, then even the most obscure changes can still hold a key to a door which might actually help me in the end.

And fear is like a lot of the natural things in life. It's not an enemy or something to be defeated. It can hinder you if you let it scare you but it can also help you as a powerful motivator. Sometimes the process and the act can be scary and sometimes even painful but the other side isn't what's scary or challenging. After everything we do, fear is the last challenge and the last stop to reaching the other side.

And more often than not, the other side is well worth it.

Chapter Six
The Golden Past

You don't necessarily realise it until you grow older and older but the past has a very peculiar allure to it, doesn't it? There's this great feeling of golden days that feel warm and bright. Everybody loves to reminisce about good times and getting nostalgic over past experience or a particular object from your past gives you the warm fuzzies inside. This part is about that feeling, the feeling of nostalgia and how it continues to be effective, especially for me who takes great indulgence in things from my past.

And, yes, I did just use the words 'Warm Fuzzies'.

Nostalgia is a powerful feeling; it can drown out anything –
Terrence Malick

As the quote just above states, Nostalgia is a powerful feeling. It's even addictive in a way. It's that warm, welcoming feeling you get when you think about the past, pretty much anything from the past. It can be places, people and objects. Nostalgia can hit different levels for different people. It all depends on their past and what they mostly relate to.

Not sure if you've noticed but a massive part of my nostalgia hit comes from pop-culture, films, shows, games. I feel nostalgic over a lot of other things as well but it's pop-culture where I often feel it the most. Over the past couple of years, nostalgia has become more and more prominent. I'm not sure if it was always there in some capacity but lately, especially this year, it has become one of the more prominent feelings in myself than any other. I guess I have to be careful with it because while nostalgia is warm, fuzzy and gives the past a golden glow, it's also kind of a trap. You lose yourself to the past when you indulge in nostalgic feelings and because you remember everything maybe a lot better than it was at the time, it's easy to keep going there, over and over again. It's safer. So it's an indulgence for sure but if you can keep your eye on the fact that you enjoy spending so much time in those safer, warmer days and moments, then I'm sure you can easily realise where you are, that being in the present moment and snap back into reality. For me it was like when I used to indulge in my own feelings of depression and hopelessness. When you are in the worst of something like that, it's easy to treat every situation and moment with a degree of hopelessness and cynicism, you indulge in the horrible feelings in your mind.

Nostalgia's the same, only instead of being dark and hopeless, it's warm and a pleasure of a state to be in. You just have to tread carefully.

But as I was saying my biggest moments of nostalgia come from pop-culture, watching stuff from when I was younger or playing games that I haven't touched since I was a lot younger. *Jurassic Park* is perhaps the best example I can give. I can watch that film time and time again and still feel like the same five-year-old I was when I first watched it. There are a couple of prime examples like that, going around to my cousin's house is another. They hit that nostalgia spot just right and it feels good every time.

Give me a bad day and I can give myself a self-deployed hit of nostalgia goodness to counterbalance it anytime. It's almost like weaponised goodness and I'm not the only one who has successfully weaponised nostalgia, speaking of the pop-culture titans I've been mentioning throughout. Each section, barring one, so far has been about a particular character or film. This section is probably going to include a whole host because if every one of these pieces of pop-culture have anything in common, it's the fact that in some way they have utilised nostalgia to some effect.

None, though, have done it more effectively than one of the defining fictional juggernauts of my life, one which I have yet to mention…

Star Wars.

I'm guessing I won't have to do that much explaining for *Star Wars*. Who hasn't seen *Star Wars*? Or at the very least, who doesn't have a general idea of what *Star Wars* is? This series has got nostalgia on stand-by, an entire saga running across three connected trilogies of film that have used nostalgia for a good two thirds of its total film number and has reaped the benefits of it every time. The original trilogy released in the late 70s and early 80s, the first and second films in that trilogy are considered to be some of the best films ever made, the third film was a fine film in its own right, just not as good as the other two. The story of Luke

Skywalker battling the evil empire enticed viewers of all ages and the films still hold together remarkably well even today.

Over 20 years after that original trilogy began, the creator, George Lucas, returned to the saga to craft an entirely new trilogy. This trilogy was set before the events of the original and would tell the story of how the feared villain, Darth Vader, came to be the infamous character almost everybody knows. Already, you could feel the sense that nostalgia was playing a part in drawing audiences back in, everybody wanted to know the story of how Vader came to be and everybody who loved the world built by George Lucas wanted to return there. Those original films were fun, emotional and a great story in general, what fan wouldn't be excited to go back?

Those warm feelings of happiness audiences had in a Galaxy far, far away could be utilised and utilised effectively. Remember the great score by John Williams? He's back to score again! Remember all the great toys? More toys are on the way! Cool looking characters? There's more! And so, the 'Prequel Trilogy' arrived with massive expectations, could that great world and story be expanded on? There's still debate on how successful that trilogy was, and yet, regardless of how you felt about the execution of those second set of films, audiences flocked to all three of them. Everybody wanted to see those final moments when the two trilogies would finally link up proper – that final moment when that small orphaned boy is looking out over those twin suns with his new parents, setting up that original film. Everybody got those nice feelings of being truly back in a place they remembered, right back to the beginning.

It was an effective tactic because it meant the new trilogy worked for all audiences. My dad and both of my uncles grew up with those original films (Both aunts to each uncle enjoyed the films as well) and so for them I'm sure it was like going back to a place they recognised, where-as for me, my brother and my cousin, the 'Prequels' were our introduction into this galaxy. We caught up with the originals while we watched the new trilogy, so that when that third film rolled around in 2005, we all got to see the saga come full circle. I was always interested in how it would feel though to see new films in the saga after already seeing some many years before. This new trilogy was new to us, so we didn't get the warm nostalgic fuzzies that my dad and uncle perhaps got.

Cut to 2015!

So, in 2015, Disney, who had purchased the rights to Lucas film, released the first in a new trilogy of films set after the original trilogy (I know, keep up) and those warm, nostalgic fuzzies that I always wondered about finally arrived within me. As a kid, I'd grown up with *Star Wars* being one of my primary sources of fun and enjoyment, so when the new Disney trilogy cranked up its marketing campaign, I was reminded of all the fun I had as a kid with *Star Wars*. And that effective nostalgia campaign that was used for the 'Prequels'. Crank that up to eleven.

Remember the great score by John Williams? He's back to score again! Remember all the great toys? More toys are on the way! Cool looking characters? There's more! Nostalgia had worked so well for the second trilogy, so why not use it again for these new films. But they went even further. Remember those real looking prosthetic designs they used for the original trilogy? We're going to use them again! Didn't like the deep politicking of the 'Prequels'? No worries, back to that old adventure style, Han Solo included!

No wonder *The Force Awakens* took over two billion dollars at the box office. The first full trailer was a full-on warhead of nostalgic potency that must have tugged at the heartstrings of everyone who had even so much as heard of *Star Wars*. People like my dad and uncles who had grown up with the originals were looking forward to seeing the old heroes again. People like me, my brother and cousin were happy for more *Star Wars* and were enjoying those feelings of nostalgia that other folks got when the 'Prequels' released back at the turn of the century. Even people who had never seen *Star Wars* before were swept up in the hype of *Star Wars'* grand return to the silver screen. It was like nostalgia was unleashed once more, only this time it took on a life of its own.

Just banking on nostalgia can have its problems though. *The Force Awakens* may have been objectively better than the 'Prequels' in a traditional film making sense but if there is one big complaint with it, then it's the fact that it's almost a carbon copy of the original film. I don't mind that it has a lot of similarities with the original *Star Wars*, I think that's what the filmmakers were going for and I get the story ideas behind doing it that way. But I guess the problem with doing it that way is that it's a structure that relies a lot on nostalgia and nostalgia is something that does eventually wear off once the initial rush has been experienced. It only takes a short time away, however, before that feeling returns. It might only take a sound or an image and you feel that warm longing for what you enjoyed in the past. *Star Wars* uses this better than no other, it always has and I'm sure it will continue to do so for as long as it is effective. Disney could release a new Luke Skywalker toy tomorrow and I'm sure fans would be out in their droves to buy it because everybody remembers how cool Luke Skywalker is, we all remember how cool *Star Wars* is, don't we?

I've mentioned *Jurassic Park* as being one of the perfect examples of giving me a strong feeling of nostalgia. Not only is it one of my favourite films of all time but it's one of the first films I remember watching, not just because it's great but because I distinctly remember hiding behind anything I could find whenever the T-Rex or the Velociraptors would appear on screen. I could rattle on about the near perfect movie that it is all day long from the animatronics to the acting, to the strangely comforting 90s aesthetic it has. On top of all that, the theme gets to me every time I hear it, if ever there was a case that a tune could represent nostalgia it would definitely be the main theme to *Jurassic Park*.

Yet while *Star Wars* uses nostalgia more as an extra device to get folks into the multiplexes, *Jurassic Park* seems to have nostalgia in its blood as a story. I think that's why it's such a nostalgic experience for a lot more people than many other films. Nostalgia is remembering things from your past in a warm, golden light and hoping to recapture that magic in the present. Sounds a little like dinosaurs, right?

Because if you haven't managed to watch *Jurassic Park* (Why?), then the plot of the film is that eccentric billionaire, John Hammond, has built a theme park where he will showcase real dinosaurs, resurrected from the dead using complex gene sequencing and other means. Everyone on Earth is fascinated by the idea of dinosaurs and so to be able to see these long-lost creatures with your own eyes would tempt even the most cynical of souls. After bringing a test group to the island, including a lawyer for legal reasons, they go about trying to patent, merchandise and sell every inch of this idea. Of course, everything goes wrong and people get eaten.

The central theme of the film is not to mess with science and don't play God. It's a cautionary tale but I think, as with most great films, anyone can apply a meaning to what they've experienced with the story and I think *Jurassic Park* is also a story of the dangers of nostalgia and becoming obsessed with the past, as much as it is a story about the dangers of playing God.

It's that sense of wonder. The first time in the film that the audience and the central characters see a dinosaur, the towering Brachiosaurus, the feeling of wonder and awe is palatable. That's what John Hammond is trying to capture at its most basic that innocent child-like feeling you get when you see something magical. He wants people to experience the same rush of joy he gets every time one of these ancient animals comes into view. There are three generations of people in the central group, John Hammond is an old man, Alan Grant is middle aged and then there is Tim Murphy, a young boy, and John Hammond's grandson. These three are perhaps the three characters most enamoured by the giant reptilian beasts and each has their moment of being star struck by them. John and Alan marvel at the Brachiosaurus while Alan and Tim are in awe of the sick Triceratops.

That obsession with the far past with these long-lost animals brought back to life is given to them in a dizzying sense of indulgence as they get to see something they thought impossible with their very own eyes. All three are nostalgic for these dinosaurs and they get exactly what they wanted with *Jurassic Park*. You know before it all goes really wrong.

I think that's where that danger of over-indulging in nostalgia comes in, especially with John Hammond. He's obsessed with getting it right, even when it's beyond saving and people are being eaten and killed by these animals. He tells a story to Ellie Sattler about 'Petticoat Lane' and a flea circus he used to put on. There were never any fleas in this 'Flea Circus' but the tight control of the tiny attractions in the circus made it look like there were. It was a careful manipulation of an illusion, all for the benefit of entertaining people, of giving that feeling of joy. He tried to recreate it with *Jurassic Park*, just on a much grander scale. Those same feelings of manufactured joy he could provide in his younger days, in his better days. Nostalgia almost kills him and everyone on the island. Well, that and one nefarious employee.

Finally, there is *Toy Story*. I've already gone over the first film in a previous section but when you look at the whole story of all four films, that's where it's continued dip into nostalgia and the feeling of youthfulness really comes into play.

You don't really see it much in the first film. It only starts to make itself apparent in the second film before really taking off in the third and fourth films. The idea is made apparent to the toys in the second film – their best times are when they are with Andy and in the second film they begin to realise that Andy will eventually outgrow them as all kids do. A kidnapped Woody is offered a place in a Japanese toy museum with a group of other toys to be admired forever. He can enjoy the admiration of kids forever but will literally be trapped by it. When he's eventually rescued by Buzz and the other toys of Andy's room, he chooses to go back because he believes that while Andy will eventually outgrow them the time they have together will be worth it.

This happens in the third film. Andy, now off to college, decides he's going to leave his toys in the attic of his house, after all, he doesn't need them anymore, not where he's going. But due to some mishap, the toys end up being donated to a day-care centre where they will be played with by a group of kids forever. The toys are still sad though, especially Woody. H he believes it was an accident and that Andy wouldn't donate them like that. He didn't but it paints Woody in a sad light as he almost refuses to believe the fact that those good times with Andy are over. He accepted the hypothetical in the previous film but struggles to experience it as something real in the third.

The toys owners become their nostalgia trap.

It adds another dimension to Buzz's journey in the first film as well. Him getting over not being a space ranger was his part in confronting this trap. When Woody can't accept that Andy might have left them at the day-care, Buzz is the first one to talk to him. He tells him to move on and to start fitting in at the day-care because he's already been through this. Buzz had to accept the fact that he is a toy, now Woody must accept the fact that Andy is moving on. The Day-care turns out to be a terrible place for the toys and after escaping and making it back to Andy's. Woody writes a note on the box to donate the toys to a young girl, Bonnie. Bonnie and the toys give each other what they need. Bonnie gets a whole box of new toys while the toys get someone who can enjoy them as they are meant to be enjoyed. They let go of their nostalgia for Andy and finally land where they are meant to be at that time.

That theme of letting go of nostalgia runs through all four films. In the first, Woody must let go of his top place with Andy and share it with Buzz. In the second the toys are confronted by the idea of Andy growing up eventually and must experience it in the third film. Finally, in the fourth film, when Bonnie starts to lose interest in Woody, he's confronted with a familiar problem and eventually decides to leave it all behind and join a group of run-away toys. Woody and the other toys struggle though this problem time and time again and only become better when they learn to grow from that longing of the better times.

Nostalgia can be tricky because it's very good at manipulating memory and past experience. It can find memories that were once good or even times that were just any old regular day and make someone long for it with a sound or an object. As much as those times may have been boring, maybe even restrictive, they have an illusion of safety. The future is uncertain and so thinking back and retreating into the familiar can be therapeutic for someone. It's because it's so warm and even tempting that you don't think of it as detrimental or even dangerous.

That's because, in a way, it isn't.

Like a lot of things in life, it's a case of too much of a good thing. Nostalgia can be harmful in large doses and it can make you long for times that weren't even as good as you think they were but I think it's important to have these anchors sometimes. I've found that while I might be a culprit in overindulging in nostalgia, I've sometimes found answers to conundrums I have in returning to something I miss. A return doesn't have to be a sign of a step backwards in the time when I needed to heal and rebuild. It was going back to the good things from my past that helped me a lot. I think it only becomes harmful when you try and replicate and give it an exclusivity that nostalgia can take too much of a hold.

That's why the longer *Star Wars* continues, the less it has to rely on nostalgia to draw people in. The criticism is already being lobbied at the newer films for overindulging in it, people love the old *Star Wars* but there's more to the Galaxy far, far away than those great memories we used to have. Even though I'm sure people would go nuts to see any of the old characters one last time. Same with the stories of John Hammond and Woody, nostalgia is a wonderful feeling in that short time it's at its best but the effect does wear off and then we have to face the unknown and the prospect of moving on.

But until then, re-watch that film, re-play that game and remember a better time. Nostalgia might be just the thing you need right now.

Home – home is where the heart is.

No matter where you've been, no matter what you've been doing, there is nothing quite like returning home. You might have spent a day working hard at wherever you happen to work or maybe you've been away for a few weeks somewhere far away, no matter the circumstance, returning home is a warm and unique feeling that usually manifests itself with a relieved sigh. It's easy to nail down the particulars of why this is, that sense of safety, of deep familiarity with your surroundings locked in from the outside world.

It's your first home, however, that really accentuates this. Some might still be living in their first home; some might have just moved out or have long been away from it but the house you grew up in usually holds a special kind of meaning for everybody, those who have left their first home behind will probably know what I mean as it often remains a safe haven for your mind even after it's just a memory. It does for me anyway.

For a lot of people, a home is just a bed, somewhere to eat and sleep before going out again into the world but for someone like me, who is naturally more insular in more ways than one, home is sometimes the only safe and comfortable place I can recognise. I'm sure everybody feels a little sad when they must leave home. It's the place they grew up in after all but the change of scenery doesn't affect them that much. Their new place of residency serves the same purpose as before, a place to sleep, a place to eat.

Leaving the house where I grew up was especially sad for me though. I remember it well, probably because it was another time where I had to let go of something I didn't really want to. It was also in that dreadful period of time I continue to mention and so maybe that made it worse but it still feels a little painful to think about that first place I called home even today. If you count both of my parents, then I'm sure I've moved to a new house about six times

131

since then. The house I spend most of my time at now is great though, it's spacious in a quiet neighbourhood and I do have my own great big room but I can't deny even that house doesn't compare to the first.

Interesting side note, whenever I dream (We'll come back to those) and it involves a house, I always, to this day, dream about my first home. None of the other six houses have ever appeared in my dreams, only ever my childhood home.

My parents have each moved away from the town where my first home was as well. My dad isn't too far out from it but it's still far enough to feel like I've even moved away from the place I went to school and played with friends. So, I guess that also makes the feeling worse, my childhood home and town trapped in this strange time capsule. It's probably nostalgia at work but those first ten years or so feel like a warmer and safer time than now and I suppose you'll say that it was meant to feel like that because that's what childhood should feel like but most people move on in their own time when they're ready. The problem is that it always feels like I left before I was ready like my time there was cut short.

It is one of the few, if only things, that I still feel a genuine sense of loss over. I've accepted and moved one from quite a few things but leaving that house is something that I still find myself thinking about late at night when I'm trying to get to sleep.

I'm sure that one day when I move into a house that will genuinely be my own house, I'll still be thinking about my childhood home and all of the things I remember from being in that house. I still wonder what it would be like if I went there today, would it look much different? How many other people have lived in it since I did? I'm guessing I wouldn't recognise it too much. I'm sure whoever has lived in it since has remodelled and redecorated every room.

But the point still stands that the connection to our childhood homes is one of the strongest there is. It's a powerful kind of nostalgia that can't really be replicated because while other things can give you a sense of nostalgia, you can always come back to them. There are plenty of films, shows and games that give me those warm nostalgic feelings but I can go back to most of them whenever I want. I'm kind of sucker for nostalgia and I'm sure it affects me a lot more than most in my inner circle. Going back to my childhood home would probably cause me to collapse.

I think that's what I'm trying to replicate now though. Like everybody, I have a lot of goals and ambitions that I want to accomplish and I think one of them might be to eventually return to that same sense of safety and equilibrium I had back in those first ten years of my life. That feeling that I could relax and be happy at pretty much any time and not have to worry about every minor thing that appeared in my head. Enjoying all these stupid things that I'd sooner write off today.

That's probably why I feel a greater sense of loss from leaving the place behind than perhaps I may have. Leaving that house meant leaving a bigger safety net than I had maybe initially recognised. There was an emotional and spiritual balance that was perfectly encapsulated in the physical walls of that home. It feels like there is a jarring divide between what it was like living there and the time after. The whole world felt safer and the town where I lived felt much more alive and as safe a place as home itself, almost just an extension of home.

When I go see my cousin on a Sunday morning, he happens to live in the same house he grew up in, the same house we always used to visit for as long as I can remember. Sometimes when I'm just sat there on one of the sofa's, I forget about everything and it almost feels as calm as it used to. The moment quickly fades away though...

For all my big ambitions of wanting to be a professional writer and scriptwriter and for all I've attempted to fix, especially regarding myself, my deepest ambition might just be to go home. I don't think I'll ever go back to that physical building in that familiar Cul-de-sac but I'm hoping I can recreate that same feeling of peace I had back then because no matter how much I enjoy a lot of things now, there is always this nagging, indescribable sense that I'm not where I should be. The more I work through my own faults and problems and check of my list of ambitions big and small, the more that feeling grows that perhaps I'm just looking to return home again.

Maybe it's this new optimistic side of me but I'm certain I will someday. I've just got this hopeful feeling that even if it looks very different to what I expect it to, I just have a funny feeling that one day I'll take a moment to myself and feel very much at home. Remembering that old house again but in a very different light. After all, you know what they say...

All roads lead to home.

And now, The Grandfather Paradox...

I hope you're all still alert and ready because I'm about to give you a question, a puzzle to solve. It is a funny time travel predicament called 'The Grandfather Paradox'. It's a little morbid so you'll have to excuse the strange circumstances of the idea. It's also really confusing, so get your best quantum physics head on.

Ready?

One day, a man successfully invents a time machine. In deciding where to go, the man decides to travel back in time to meet his grandfather when he was much younger. Due to extraordinary circumstance, the time traveller inadvertently ends up killing his grandfather. He also went so far back that his grandparents hadn't yet conceived either the time traveller's mother or father, whichever parent they eventually conceive.

The problem is that now the traveller's grandfather is dead, that means the time traveller was never born as his grandparents never conceived one of his parents. But that's not even the biggest and most confusing problem. The real paradox comes in when you realise that if the time traveller killed his grandfather and was erased from existence...

How, then, did the time traveller go back and accidentally kill his grandfather?

I'm not sure there is an answer, the man goes back, kill his grandfather. So, he's never born but if he's never born, then he can't go back. So, his grandfather must still be alive! But if his grandfather is still alive, the man must be born, surely? But then, surely, he goes back and well then, he must accidentally...

And around and around and around.

Apparently, this is called a Causal Loop, something happening in an infinite loop that can't really be solved. Time travel is awesome. Theoretically, it's stuff like this that makes me really interested in time travel and quantum physics. Yeah, it's fun to think about the simple things like, what if met this famous historic figure? But I love when it gets incredibly complex and you really start to comprehend (Or not) the mind-bending consequences of even the simple act of going backwards in time or forwards.

I think one of the problems with a legitimate sense of time travel though would be how selfishly people would use it. Not just the idiot who would go back to win the lottery because they want all the money but people who genuinely understand the dire consequences of changing things regardless of how terrible they may have been at the time. We've seen it in films like *Back to the Future*, they're fun films but they're constantly warning about the dangers of changing things, how even the smallest action can cause irreversible damage.

The problem is that I think in the end people would just ignore the conscience and their instinct. They would probably do whatever it takes to change a past outcome, the urge would be just too strong and they would end up doing it anyway. Even the best of us would be too tempted to stop global atrocities or even personal tragedy.

It's an interesting hypothetical to ponder at any time. Think of one bad thing in your life. Could you go back and change it? Should you?

I've thought about it plenty of times. Especially in the moment when it seems to be at its worst and most immediate. I think about if I had a time machine and if I could change the circumstances surrounding the event to prevent it but not only could the consequences of that action be worse than anyone could imagine but the minutia of details surrounding the initial incident could be so numerous it would take years to sort out one tiny problem.

Have you guessed where I'm going with this?

I keep coming back to the events of late 2008 but as I've said they have in a multitude of ways, directed, influenced and been a major influence on my life ever since. They've given me severe anxiety, depression, a set of deep-seated fears and caused a lot more problems than I care to mention. So, would I go back and try and change the events if I could, regardless of consequence?

No. Never.

If I had a perfectly working time machine, I would absolutely not go back and change any event, including the worst in my memory. One reason, if this wasn't already apparent, is because I think time travel is more trouble than it's worth. The other reason is because I think everything is meant to happen for a reason, that as troubling as times can get, there is an eventual benevolence to what transpires that, eventually, we all come to understand and accept.

You've all heard of hindsight, right? I think I've even mentioned it already somewhere in here. I think hindsight itself is a form of time travel, an ability to look back on past events, good and bad, in a new light. As I've said, most people would probably look to use time travel for selfish ways, there may be good intentions involved but at the end of the day they would be looking to eradicate pain, regret and other negative emotions. The temptation would be too strong not to go back and not say that horrible thing to help that person instead of ignoring them.

But while we can't actually time travel (We really shouldn't), we can look back with hindsight and forgive or forget. There are a lot of reasons I'd go back and change a lot of things but they're selfish reasons for the benefit of me and I should be better than that. It's easy to see a terrible circumstance as just that and not see that even the worst of things can eventually produce something beautiful. I'm a much better and stronger person now. I've had help, mainly therapy, but there is this small part of me that thinks maybe everything was meant to happen. I might be thinking a little more optimistically but I believe that even though there have been some bad times, there is some kind of payoff coming.

I've said that in that horrible time I started to get the idea I wanted to be a professional writer to use my creativity in a constructive way. Maybe that's the trade-off for everything that happened. That the bad times will eventually make way for greater times, and that the struggle and emotional hardship I had to endure were necessary to make me into the person I wanted and needed to be.

What if I did go back and change things? And then I became something totally different, I know that because of time travel I'd never know any different, but the thought is scary. My personal ambition is something which I hold very dear and something I hold in high regard as one of my greatest strengths and as one of the cornerstones of my identity. The more I think about how I've changed and how I've grown from experiences good and bad, the more I reject the idea of time travel and changing things. Everything, in its own way, is how it should be. You can hate it, disagree with it and that is fine but in the end, when we're all ready to pass on to whatever is next, I'm sure we'll all be able to agree that every moment is a piece of us. Even something that was communal is a part of us as a person and in the end was tailor made for our journey through life.

It's fun to think about going back, meeting your family when they were young, a famous historical figure in their prime but when you catch yourself thinking about changing the past, about that time when something went very wrong and it caused you great pain, purge the thought. It's not yours to change. Instead, try and look back and see how it has moulded you into something more than what you were. It may be difficult and painful but there is strength to be found in suffering and pain. I ignored it for years. It was only when I was forced to look back on it in a neutral light. Seeing it for what it was I saw how it had and still could, change me for the better.

I know that some pains and experiences will be much worse than mine and that changing them might be the only option in that hypothetical instance but we can't change things in the past and maybe we shouldn't. We can be better people by learning to grow from whatever happened.

And can you imagine how messy it would get if everybody went back changing things? God only knows what would happen, the universe would probably short circuit or something.

So, if you take anything away from this section, it's that you shouldn't go back to meet your younger grandfather.

You might just change more than you hoped...

Chapter Seven
The One. The Many. And Beyond.

We edge out into different territory in this section. It's about even bigger ideas than what's been presented so far, like the individual and the collective, and how the two are in a constant tug of war with one side maybe having too much of an edge at the moment…but aside from that, it's also about someone I hold very dear and then about ideas too big and strange to often comprehend.

I know it's a bit of an odd mix.

Pub? – Multiple Characters in Shaun of the Dead

My dad loves the pub. He loves going down on a Sunday evening after a long week at work and I often join him and the (Ever-growing) group that gather almost every Sunday. Another thing he's very fond of are movies about World War II. Doesn't matter what part of World War II, if it's part of that period of time, he'll happily sit down and watch.

But this section isn't about my dad in particular. It's about the pub, about World War II and how they are connected, as well as Individualism and collectivism and solidarity. Yeah, it's a scattershot section but I promise it will make sense, hopefully.

Individualism and collectivism are two interesting terms. If I had to apply myself to one, it would definitely be individualism. I've always believed in the power of the individual over the collective. For better or worse, one person and individual can change or derail any plan or action. No matter how big a group or organisation, a singular mind can cause something great or terrible to happen. Even the idea of the collective surely starts with the individual, right?

From what you've probably and hopefully read so far, I'm sure you'll agree that I'm more suited as someone who believes in individualism. I'm not going to shun the collective, however. The collective can often achieve what the individual cannot. The individual can come up with an idea or a cause but it often takes more than one person to truly see a vision come to pass. That's where the collective comes in but, as I've banged on about in most of the sections you've read, a balance is needed between the two. Unfortunately, I don't think that balance is there at the minute. Maybe it's the specific environment I've grown up in and currently live in but there seems to be a sense that collectivism is more prominent and maybe even preferred than individualism.

It's almost like the whole discussion about introverts and extroverts again except this isn't just to do with how a person deals with the world in a social sense. This is about a lot more than that. As I thought about this section (This entire thing was very 'on the fly'), I realised that this section sort of brings together a lot of the previous points I've made, it's kind of as close to a summary or even a conclusion as I could get without forcing it. Nostalgia, wants and needs, introversion and extroversion, remembering who you are, they all seem to coalesce some way into this idea and in a way, kind of put a broad underline on what it's all been about for me. This whole wild ride that's lasted over a decade.

So, who is more important? The individual or the collective?

Here's a fun fact about me; up until recently, I didn't know that the word pub was short for public house. You know because a pub is basically just a big house for lots of people, also known as the public, to meet and talk. My mini mind was blown. That's right, the guy throwing words like individualism and collectivism at you, didn't know that pub was short for public house. We're all clever and stupid in our own ways.

But, as I was saying, I go to the pub on a Sunday with my dad, my step mum and their group of friends, which seems to be getting larger and larger by the way. I swear they find someone new every month. Not everyone makes it every week but whenever there is an event on in the village, everybody tries to make it and so I'm sure soon they won't be classified as a group but be promoted to 'Mob'. When they're all in there on a Sunday evening, they won't just talk to each other but they'll converse with pretty much everyone in the pub and I mean everyone. Maybe this is why the group is so big.

Seriously, nearly everybody in the pub talks to each other, everyone has their own groups per se but at this point they might as well just all combine into one. The pub and its people, at least the ones on a Sunday, might as well represent the village. Everyone who goes in, lives in the village and so the communal feeling of the village is condensed into one building. Usually as well between the different conversations the group will have, I'll often hear them mention that so and so isn't in tonight or someone needs to see a certain someone about something or other. There's never really a lone drinker in the pub, they usually either belong to a group already or are encouraged to join one.

It's one of the best and most personal examples of collectivism I can think of. There's a sense of warmth to this idea that a whole village can collate in one building. that almost everybody knows each other and it comes off as noticeably strange to one group or more when certain people don't appear for even one week. It's a feeling and an experience that most try and recreate every week because just like with nostalgia, there is a warm and safe feeling to that repeating achievement of community every week.

And yet, like nostalgia, it's not all good because nothing in life is wholly good. It can't be.

Before I go any further, I'd like to mention that this section was very tricky to write because it's probably the only section where I perhaps tread into an area of presumptuousness. It's the one area where the subject doesn't just involve the experiences and relation of things to me, it is partly about the collective after all. And so, if some of my thoughts seem out of place, then just know I tried to be as fair and reasonable as possible.

That communal feeling that is oft replicated can seem a lot like nostalgia because both seem to have a hidden element of being slightly addictive to reach. I can see why it would be as desirable as the dive into nostalgia because it has this lofty level of connectiveness to it. Everybody knows each other, everybody's here for a drink and a good time. It can almost feel like an end goal. The problem, I think, with this is that the more of a communal and collective feel everybody aims for, the more of the same people look for. It seems logical, right? The more common ground there is, then the more everybody will feel closer together and safer together. So, everyone aims to expand the collective through that because then that sense of community will be tighter and stronger.

After all, we're all in this together, aren't we?

But like nostalgia, this dive into a larger familial feel can be more constant then anyone realises, to the point where the dive can be almost never-ending. It's the same with nostalgia, the sensation is warm, inviting and safe and yet linger too long in it and you may as well be the same as the memories that you like to indulge in. The more I write this, I realise the more it sounds like this is all a bad thing, I'm a fan of individualism and am probably sounding biased towards it. But it's not all bad, just like it's not all good. It's that slight danger of overindulgence and teetering over the edge.

Sit there long enough, taking in the environment every week and you realise that the conversations and the habits they sometimes blend. It's one of the dangers of the collective, you start to draw so much strength and positivity from the communal dynamic that you lose sight of when the individual is kind of drowned out and it becomes strange when something different arrives. My poor little brother does sometimes get some strange looks when he sits there with his soft drink.

An interesting contrast is when I go out with my best friend and meet up for a drink at a different pub nearby, there isn't that huge group dynamic in the other pub, it's not just me and my friend sat quietly drinking and chatting, everybody there mainly keeps to themselves. Coming from the other pub it can seem kind of jarring but after spending more time there, it has a pleasantly different feel. It feels more like the people there are almost like 'ships in the night', they're there to meet up with someone, have a quiet drink and depart. Yet, to the community at the neighbouring pub it would probably be off-putting rather than just having this different vibe.

It circles back to the extravert and introvert argument (I'm telling you. It circles back to everything). The world sees the extravert as the prime position as they are more socially tuned and the world is a social place but it's only as time has gone on that people have started to see that while introverts are outnumbered, they are no less important.

Let me put it to you this way, one pub is like an old medieval tavern with plenty of drinking, laughing and joyousness. The other is like a saloon from the old American west, it's quieter but from the experience I've had there, people more or less like it that way. The problem with collectivism and how this represents it is that it's such a positive feeling that it starts to meld and become a deceptively natural end point rather than just another way of life. It's joyous, safe and makes it feel like everybody is one but take it too far and everybody does become one but sometimes the best groups and the best communities are the ones made up of the most diverse individuals.

But if individuals form habits, then community births tradition and tradition is looked upon as a proud institution. So, it bears repeating, it's not all bad if it works especially well at one thing, it's that in being a part of it for one night, you forget about all those little problems. Rampant individualism can be just as bad, trust me I know. Everybody needs somebody. It's just don't let it go too far. I've learnt that different is good after all. Either way, pubs are pretty good one way or another.

Moving swiftly on, I mentioned that my dad also loves watching World War II films. World War II is an interesting time period because while it's one of the most horrific time periods in human history, I often see it romanticised in film and other media. It could just be a way of making sure we don't forget that era in a positive way. We see all the heroics of the folks that bravely fought for their country while at the same time keeping it all fresh in our minds so we don't repeat something as world shattering as a World War ever again. Thankfully, we haven't had a World War III. I hope we never do and that we've grown as a race to do better than to descend into that level of conflict.

But films about this period are often great, some of the greatest films ever made are about World War II and they often hit the right emotional spot in showing the heroics and the bravery of both the one man and the country because when the war hit, everybody did their part. Men, women and children, all had a part to play in stopping the axis of evil. It's the ultimate standard bearer for the idea of the collective – there was no hesitation, people dove in and did their part.

The world was at stake, not just your own country but everywhere. It was a time when, for the most part, it was easy to discern right from wrong. The world was dangerous and frightening but everybody could easily stand together when faced with something so close to being, well, evil.

I think that's why some people nowadays have a strange fondness of the era. One side of the conflict performed unforgivable, irredeemable actions that have left scars that are still felt today but when people think about the way the other side of the conflict banded together on a global level, you can't help but get a good feeling. This was action without hesitation into almost certain death and no one wanted to let that slide. In a very broad sense, it was a simpler time.

And that might be a problem a lot of people have with the modern age. The twenty-first century is complicated and a lot of things in every facet of life have changed as they do in every period of time. As much as some people might want to think this, it's become a lot deeper than just right and wrong. The modern information age means we can gain access to news and other info at an alarmingly fast rate and so the world seems a lot morally greyer than it did. World War II had its morally complex moments, I'm sure, but we remember the heroics and the daring do most of all, or at least we like to.

Sometimes it feels like everybody wants to go back then to escape the more morally and socially complex world we live in now. It's not that today's world is bad, we have had a long time of general peace. It's just even I'll admit it become more difficult to navigate and what we think is the right choice may not be so right at all. Right and wrong is a basis for decision making, not the all, end all of what you should choose to decide. Right and wrong appears to create a safety net for how you should react. I'm not saying that thinking along the lines of right and wrong is in itself wrong but as you get older and you mature, I think it's more about choice and consequence.

I think people end up getting a little nostalgic for that time period because it is often presented as a time of simplicity in what everybody did. We see the stories presented to us and see that there were so many definitive decisions and choices but while it appears to have been easier and simpler, I think the reality was that it was just what everybody had to do. Propaganda worked effectively, really effectively, to galvanise nations of people into fighting for whatever great cause they found themselves on and the stories we see presented on film or in books often romanticise the actions of the time. But it was only simpler because choices became narrowed and even removed in a time of world-shattering conflict. It seems better because in hindsight we know what we'd all do but like nostalgia is want to do when presenting its warm glow, you forget how terrifying the time must have been for everybody.

That doesn't diminish the achievements of the collective force though. It was a remarkable achievement of propaganda, human spirit and effort that showed how powerful the collective could be when it's fighting for a common, easily definable goal. I guess the rose-tinted glasses make it seem like that's the ultimate goal of unity we should be striving for, even though it was all of the time and times have changed.

But even if it often looked as one of the best examples of the collective rising to the challenge, it was also a time when the individual mattered just as equally. That's why it's so fascinating to hear a new story from anybody from that time. A soldier, an officer, a prisoner or someone on the home front, everybody mattered as equally as the other and their differences were used to contribute to the greater conflict on a whole. It was a perfect marriage of the individual and the collective, probably one of the reasons why it's often remembered in a romantic light. The triumphs and the victories were of the varying individuals standing as one, spurred on by the calls of the others at their back.

Like I said, the best groups are those made of the most diverse individuals.

So I guess it's easy to see why people would, in a way, get a little nostalgic for the era. Everybody mattered but if the people around you get nostalgic for the times, then it's another side of life that gets nostalgic for the propaganda machines that were in full force back in the day because those propaganda tactics were effective, weren't they? It may have been the best use of propaganda I've ever seen. It drummed up support of all kinds in a way which has never really been replicated. Although I've been witness to some attempts in doing so, not by the country mind you but by businesses.

And, no, this isn't me taking another shot at my workplace – more of a pat on the head. Swing and a miss kind of thing.

Businesses are focused on profits and money, naturally. So it must seem kind of lucrative at the way propaganda so successfully drummed up a nation to use their greatest efforts in times of such need except that was against world domination and the closest you can get to an evil dictatorship. It's a far cry from a business.

But bless their hearts they tried.

In 2018, the whole store gathered at a very nice hall to meet up and get some questions answered, as well as hear about any plans going forward. Safe to say for varying reasons, morale wasn't at its highest and as was explained, things weren't likely to get a whole lot better. I think people were hoping for a minor miracle, which didn't happen and the higher-ups tried their best to explain why. And while it was kind of a bummer to hear that things were likely to continue along the same trajectory, I could get why.

But for me, it wasn't that that bothered me. Businesses are focused on profits and so they're always going to try and save money anyway they can, at least they were honest about it at the meeting. The thing that bothered me was how they tried to galvanise everybody to work harder and better. There was a company made video with employees grinning and saying great things with an uplifting song in the background, a montage of inspirational and famous speeches and I swear one of the higher ups did the fist pump gesture.

I would have rolled my eyes but they would've gone so far into the back of my head you'd have to send search and rescue to get them back.

The point is you can't replicate that kind of spirit from before. Not only does it apply to the moment, it applies to the fact that it was used against a far different reason. That kind of tactic is overt and on-the-nose but it worked because that's what people needed when they had little hope of survival. They could have played the 'but it is your job' card but thankfully they either thought better of it or just didn't think of it at all. And even if that statement is true, isn't it all in pursuit of a cynical goal?

Businesses are focused on money and profit, naturally. It's kind of hard to rally the troops when at the end of the day you're just asking people to muster more energy for a goal they don't truly benefit from. Not only that but in trying to rally us all, they made sure to make good use of the word 'one' in front of anything. You know, like one team which works in making everyone feel involved but forgets why it worked so well back then because it didn't forget the individual.

Like I said, back then, as much as it was the greatest group effort, each person brought their own to the table. They were all soldiers and fighters on every front but it was their personalities and their single traits that made it all so special. The more the place tries to galvanise us as a group and a collective, the more it loses sight of how you utilise each person as an individual. It's the problem with the collective on a bigger level than the joyousness of the pub community. Keep trying to reenergise people under the idea of a whole and people's identity will work hard to align with that collectivism. Then individuality and identity can be lost and identity is someone's greatest source of humanity.

But I guess it was a good effort and maybe their hearts were in the right place. Maybe.

Individualism and collectivism isn't something that should be chosen outright. There is a place for both and both have their dangers of overindulgence and of going too far. An individual needs the collective to help achieve goals and to feel a sense of unity and the collective mustn't forget that each individual with each identity is what made it what it is. They must be balanced, just like everything else in life.

But there is one more thing this argument applies to, something which I've mentioned a few times already and is where this argument finally comes back to a more personal level. I mentioned that one of the benefits of the collective is that it offers a lot more safety than the individual. Being in such a strong and numerous group is sure to make anyone feel better and warmer but safety does not necessarily equate to happiness and the traditions of the collective are sometimes at odds with the individual, especially with how an individual can change over time.

The beliefs, the ambitions and the aspirations of the collective might not correspond with the individual and so the individual must make a choice. One that might not necessarily be right or wrong but has more to do with their personal fulfilment and overall happiness, even if it riles the collective up.

As I was writing this, it instinctively made me think about my choice in pursuing writing along with other life choices I've made so far. They aren't exactly the norm and plenty of people have questioned why I've made these choices. They're not traditional choices that people usually make, they're less safe and more strange I suppose but they are what I've chosen because I believe it is in my best interest and hope that it will all make sense, not just for me but for everybody else someday. But it also made me think of something else, especially in regards of tradition and people's ingrained, albeit good intentioned beliefs.

It made me think of my parent's divorce. It's one of the most, if not the most, traumatic event I've experienced and it's caused me numerous problems over the years. I've always thought of it in a negative light, regardless of how things have turned out, and have only ever associated it with fear, anger or disdain while I won't go into the details of the how's or the what's writing about the complexness of the individual and the collective, as well as thinking about how my career choice goes against people's traditional idea of careers, I actually came to a sort of mini epiphany.

I actually thought of the event in a strangely positive light. Maybe all of this has been about breaking tradition and staking new ground. The individual vs. the collective is an ever-changing battle and sometimes it isn't so simple, maybe it doesn't apply to right or wrong.

And so, after therapy, after clearing my mind and thinking about how my choices have been about an individual turning their back on the entrenched beliefs of the collective, as good-natured as they may be. I finally came to see something traumatic in a surprising light.

Inspiring.

Pantheon – A group of particularly respected, famous or important people.

I've made mention to a lot of things so far in this. Between personal tragedies, beloved characters, long held hobbies and the general journey I've been on, I've covered a lot of ground that I intended and find myself just about ready to wrap this up.

But before we do eventually come to the end, I'd like to mention one more person. I've talked about larger-than-life characters like Batman, Iron Man and Buzz Light-year.

Heroes who are capable of dizzying feats of bravery and inspire generations of people but there is one last inspiring presence to cover – one final person to give proper credit to.

My granddad, Mick.

Michael was his full name but me and the rest of my family always called him Mick. I don't think he minded. Unfortunately, he passed away on New Year's Day of 2009. There was a lot going on at the time and going through quite a bit myself, I don't think I processed the whole thing very well or properly at all. It was only years later, maybe even a decade later when I really started to understand the loss I felt. The more time goes on, the more I miss him. He is, so far, the only close family to have passed away. Everybody else is, thankfully, still here.

If I had to describe how I think of him, it would be in a way that in a lot of different ways often gets dismissed as detrimental. I put him on a pedestal of being something greater than perhaps he was or could ever really be but as for how I remember him, he remains atop that pedestal, probably forever.

That's what's interesting about family in a way. We all put our parents, grandparents and other members of our family on pedestals for a long time. When we're born into this world, we are, hopefully, cared for and loved by our families. They try to do everything in their power to give us what we need and often want. Sometimes you can be spoiled with things but I think that even being a little spoilt sometimes is ok, as long as it's not too much.

This all comes with a Catch 22 though. In providing such a deep and loving amount of care for your children, they end up putting their families on that pedestal.

Eventually, you come to learn that even though your family gave you everything they could, they are still just people. They're just as human as you are with wants, needs and dreams. People who also make mistakes and can be subject to errors but people, nonetheless.

The time when they descend from that pedestal can be different for everyone – the circumstance and timing can be all different. For me, it was during the time when my parents split up. I've mentioned before how I couldn't comprehend my parents going through that because of how I was so secure in my idea of their marriage being an institution in and of itself but when they did, emotions were high and due to the hardships of that process, I learned that all across my family, everybody was capable of divulging their worst impulses. Words were said that I never thought I'd hear from the people that had cared for me and my brother and sometimes, they'd sink into places I never thought I'd see.

Up until this point, my family had rules and beliefs that nobody would ever swear or curse in front of us, nobody would ever say a bad thing about anybody when we were around. On top of all the usual things that you should do around children, this put my family squarely on top of that pedestal. The care, the love, the attention, these people were the great providers and I idolised them all as anybody fairly would.

But after that devastating event, I started to see the other side of them, what they were like when everything was crumbling and everything looked a lot bleaker. In a lot of ways, it can create resentment and a distance. Everybody has to take their parents and their family off their pedestals eventually but I assume for a lot of people it happens naturally as they grow. For me, it happened all at once in a time when emotions were sky high. I relied on my family for everything, and soon transform into someone who had to start to care for himself was a little jarring. I've gone over it before but I essentially shut down.

I didn't get it – I didn't even really like it. These people had done everything to care for me and my brother and now they've all turned on each other, saying and doing things I didn't want to see or hear. I still had them on that pedestal, even when they'd leapt down themselves. It took years during my time in therapy before I properly took them from that pedestal myself. Yeah, they'd been down for a while but I still wanted them to be up there.

I failed to see them as human beings.

Once I went through my time in therapy, cleared my mind and saw the world in a mature light, I started to see my family less as the great providers they once were and more the humans they had always been, that made me appreciate them a lot more.

These people had given up their time, their wants and needs, all to give me something. Whether it was time or money or even the basics like food and shelter, everybody had given up something to take good care. It makes taking them off that pedestal worth it. I even appreciated all the little things they did even more, all those rules about no swearing in front of us. It's small, nobody had to do it but they did.

Leaving them up there on the pedestal you and they create when you are born and are growing up makes you have a constant expectation. They should do this for me, they should do that. They never had to, they just did. When you realise that, when you take a moment to think about what small and large sacrifices they made to care for you and give you what you needed, you really appreciate them more. Even when you've grown up and have taken much more responsibility yourself, they still only ask for some time together, which is a fair trade if you ask me.

Yes, they are your family and should be the most important people to you but they're also human. They have their own desires, their own faults and their own set of characteristics that make them much more interesting than just who you initially found them to be. It's nobody's fault; they are on that pedestal for so long, it's part of the job. Just remember when they come down and they will come down eventually, that they gave a lot for you. So, when they do something that shocks you or upsets you, remember them as people just like you.

The thing about my granddad though is that he never really came down from that pedestal. He passed away just as things were starting to get bad. So, the only memories and experiences I have with him are only the upmost positive ones. There was never a moment where I saw the actual human side of him, which isn't meant to be a bad thing. Everybody else has gradually shown their flaws and their mistakes like I said they are no longer on that pedestal. They're as human as anyone else and I don't see them as these infallible providers anymore, which is good because nobody can do that forever and it brings you and them onto a level field.

Because my granddad passed away before that transition started to happen, he still remains the only one on that pedestal. I never saw his flaws or his truly human moments,

157

he ate one too many biscuits and fell asleep a lot but he was always exactly what you needed him to be. He'd tell us a story, make us a drink and watch cartoons with us. I'm sure if I learnt more about him from my other family members, then maybe there would be flaws and characteristics about him that I never saw or heard but I don't want to. I honestly want him to stay exactly where he is, atop that beaming pedestal.

I've said that you should appreciate what your family did before they eventually came down because the effort was all their own. In a way, they had no obligation to do anything they did for you and so any act of good from them becomes more altruistic when you realise they gave up time and effort to do it. This has made me appreciate my granddad even more recently because while I only remember him up until the end of my childhood, I remember him for being kind, caring, patient and funny. Maybe it's just the golden memories talking but there seemed to be an honesty to the way he was as well, of course, family are obligated to be good to each other but it seemed to be a natural state for him.

I honestly believe that if I was to ever find out more about him, these qualities wouldn't change much if at all.

People often talk about how sons and daughters take after members of their family, usually their parents. How they grow up and take on their qualities, obviously because they're biologically connected to each other. I've always wondered whether it was true, whether anybody really had a choice in it, do they do it because, subconsciously it's a safety mechanism? Following on from your parents, kind of like carrying on their legacy through their habits and mannerisms.

I don't know if we choose to do that but if we do, then I guess I've come to realise that I carry a lot on from my granddad. I think I may have taken on more than I realise. He was a patient man. I never saw him argue or fight. I've always resolved to solve everything with a patient heart. He had a garden he loved to take care of, he was slow and considerate in taking care of it when I went through therapy, I made sure to be slow and considerate in my actions. It meant everything got the right amount of effort. He was also consistently kind and compassionate. I don't know if he was ever in a bad mood because he was always good to me, my brother and my cousin. I try and be good to everyone now, even if I'm frustrated at work or in a low mood, it's not other people's fault.

My granddad, Mick, wasn't even my biological grandfather. My biological grandfather, George, passed away before I was born. From what my dad and my grandma tell me, it's almost like my granddad Mick appeared out of nowhere when they were in most need of him. It's almost magical to think about. It's like he just appeared and took care of everybody, eventually taking care of me, my brother and my cousin as well.

The more time goes on and the older I get, the more I'm amazed by him.

But that's not to discount the efforts of everybody else. They may have gradually become much more like regular people, people with flaws and characteristics we may not agree on but they're still family. Family who dedicated what they could to taking care of us. It's an admirable quality they still all share, even in regard to what has happened.

They are a wonderful pantheon of people.

Yet there is still one who sits high up on that pedestal and he'll never come down because I don't want him to. He's a man who I've come to hold in exceptionally high regard and hope to carry on the good qualities he showed every day to me and others and when I do eventually pass on to the great beyond...

I'll look for him first.

There's mysterious forces at work – a thousand different characters from a thousand different stories.

Before we reach the very end, I thought after all the heavy emotion of the preceding sections, we could all do with something a little lighter to finish on. I've made an attempt, for better or worse, to understand everything I can so far in my life. From the whys to the whos to the whats, I've often had an urge to just know but even the smartest, most attuned people on Earth can't understand everything and eventually we will all hit that invisible wall of mystery.

Dreams are something which nobody quite understands. There are some scientific meanings to the idea of dreaming but then there are also a lot of spiritual meanings to go along with that. When we are in deep sleep, completely gone from the world, we dream – incredible, terrifying, sometimes euphoric, dreams are like stories that we directly take part in. They are somewhere we travel when we are unconscious from the waking world and to some, it can be something to quite look forward to. Plenty of people go on about how they are looking forward to getting some sleep for the benefit of rest and recharging their bodies but dreams are also another reason to look forward to it.

I used to have a lot of nightmares when I was younger. I'd dream of terrifying experiences where I'd run into horrifying monsters that would jolt me awake. I didn't used to enjoy dreaming because of this and would hope I'd sleep through the night without being transported to another frightening hell scape. Gladly though, I've come to enjoy dreaming far more since growing up. I have more pleasant dreams now and even when they aren't happy dreams, there are just odd or funny. I rarely get nightmares anymore, although I suppose even the nightmares have lost their power now that I've gotten older. The scary monsters aren't so scary anymore.

The problem with dreams now though is that as much as I enjoy their spiritual quality and hidden meanings, I quickly forget about them when I wake up. Even if I put effort into holding onto the memory of the dream, it soon slips away even before I've made my morning coffee. There is one, however, that has stuck with me for a while now, it's the only dream to have ever lingered. I wonder if there's a reason why.

It's night, pitch black outside. I'm standing on a pier, waiting to climb aboard a boat. It's only a small boat, a wooden rowing boat that must only be for me. I'm not sure how I know but I know it's headed for 'Paradise' wherever that may be. I'm anxious, stressed and frightened, just as I'm about to climb aboard, something roars at me. It's not long before I'm being chased across the pier by a monstrous being. It's like a great ape, layered in shadow, roaring and out to get me. It's like it doesn't want me to board the boat. I'm chased around before I circle back around and head back towards the rowing boat, the monster not far behind. Before I reach the boat or the monster reaches me, the dream ends.

I remember telling my first therapist about it. They were interested in if I had any vivid dreams and so I described to them this particular one especially considering how much it had stuck with me. They asked me what I thought it meant, all dreams have some meaning after all. I said I didn't know, I couldn't think what it could mean, why it lingered in my mind. My therapist had their own theory on what it meant but they never told me, they said it was important that I came to my conclusion on such a vivid dream without outside influence.

Me, a boat, a monster, who knows what it could really mean. Maybe someday in the future, it will all become clear. For now, though, it remains a mystery.

As much as that dream was strange, I still enjoy dreaming, seeing what mad and unexpected place I turn up to every night. Some of them are stronger than others, some nights I've dreamt of somewhere so convincing that I'm taken by surprise when I wake up like I almost confused the two realities. Sometimes that can be far more than just surprising though. Sometimes it can even be disappointing, especially when I dream of things that could've been like my dreams are playing a cruel trick on me.

I've mentioned already that I always end up dreaming of my childhood home in a situation where home appears. No other house, just the one I grew up in. Its dreams like that that can leave me with disappointment when I finally wake up. I enjoy where I live currently and am happy there but

162

every so often my dreams will remind me how much I miss that old house but it's not only that, I've dreamed of a hundred other happy situations and moments that I know I'll never have for one reason or another only to wake up to the world I'm in. It's hard not to feel disappointed and when I'm waking up at 5 o'clock in the morning for work, the disappointment only sets in harder. After all, I was only just convinced I was living my best life, only to open my eyes to the sound of an alarm and the pitch black of the cold morning. Minutes later, I've forgotten the dream altogether.

Aside from that, it's the feelings you get when you're inside the dream that can really bring it together. Have you ever dreamt you could fly? The feeling you get when you soar through the air is indescribable. Humans can't fly and so when you manage to do it in a dream, it's like a feeling you've never felt before, maybe a feeling you're not supposed to feel.

It's strange. I suffer from severe anxiety and so I find it hard to relax and keep my mind still. I've been told I'll probably suffer with it for the rest of my life that I have to live with the constant anxiousness. It's like I'm constantly looking over my shoulder for something that isn't even there, wide-eyed for danger when it doesn't even exist. Even when I'm sat doing absolutely nothing at home, I can't escape the feelings of anxiety. When I dream of home, however, it's the only time I ever experience peace. I don't just mean putting your problems aside and relaxing like people can do, I mean real peace of mind – a feeling of weightlessness that I never feel in real life. That's the problem with anxiety, those times are probably the only time I'll ever feel like that.

Everything in life has its shortcomings, even dreams. When I was young, I was scared of every dream I had at night, now I'm older. I just end up disappointed at leaving the dream world behind. Even when I'm being chased by monsters in the dead of night, they've transformed into the most ideal place, maybe they'll transform again later down the line.

But until then, I can only keep on dreaming and hope that one day they'll make sense and have genuine meaning. They are a mysterious part of life among other things and I've come to appreciate the many mysterious that we can't explain. I'm not talking about conspiracy theories or wacky ideas, just the sense that sometimes, things don't make sense and we just have to play along. I've said that years ago, I started to believe in something greater and that I had the idea that something more powerful is pulling the strings in one way or another. I still believe that.

Just like we can't explain dreams, we also can't really explain how we came to be over everything else or what is beyond death. We'll always strive to figure out these answers, the big answers to the big questions that have resonated throughout the ages. Maybe we aren't meant to figure out these things and we should accept and learn to trust things that are out of our grasp. As much as I've often been driven to find answers to the many questions and problems I've had, I keep getting the feeling that, in the end, I should trust life. Everybody says in times of need or trouble that things will work out, as if waiting and trusting or the solution to whatever individual problem someone is facing. It's simple but true, patience and a clearer mind do help to find solutions to problems but what if they're really is something we can't explain, turning the cogs to help us. That would be something.

Everybody worries and thinks of a myriad of issues every day. Small, trivial things that fill adult life to the brim and make you forget about the things that you miss all the time. I spent some time away from the world and in that time, I realised that you could be amazed by even the simplest of things. You can think of a hundred questions about how something works or why something happened at that exact time and most of the time people will answer with that's just how life works. It's an interesting answer because when you stop and think about it, you realise that life is so massive and complex, way beyond just our planet, that for life to 'just work', there must be something more at play to make sure it does work.

Especially in moments of coincidence or déjà vu, when the cracks in the glass almost show, when it's like you almost get a glimpse of something else going on. It's that I've come to love and appreciate. The idea that the worst and best luck, the most volatile or euphoric of experiences can happen because of something mysterious that's flowing just beyond what we understand. People sometimes wave it all off as randomness, maybe in a hope of coping with the pendulum of feelings you get in differing situations but that's too easy, isn't it?

Like with dreams, maybe one day it will all make sense and somebody will get the answers to all of the questions they've ever had. Every coincidence will have a reason and every terrible moment will be worth something in the long run, maybe we'll have to wait until we pass on to find out.

Until then, I say we trust the mystery.

Pass on what you have learned…

When writing about Batman and his power as a symbol I mentioned that *The Dark Knight Rises* was my personal favourite film ever. I also mentioned that from that film, the scene in which Bruce climbs out of the pit he'd been trapped in was perhaps my favourite scene from any film, ever. I think that scene is only my favourite because it has the rest of the film backing it up. It's a fine scene on its own but it's the context and build-up of the previous films and scenes that lend it its final emotional punch as far as my favourite scene on its own…

There is another.

I always find myself debating between two scenes, the one I've already mentioned and another. I think it's always such a close toss up because the two scenes are quite similar in what they represent and the idea at their heart. They both affirm the power and potency of belief, self-belief especially. Whereas one scene takes place at the end of one character's journey, another takes place at the beginning, cementing the idea of belief as something that waxes and wanes from person to person and even from a singular person's life more often than not.

Positive self-belief can be a powerful force, it can propel us and motivate us to accomplish great deeds and reach higher levels of fulfilment, so how do we gain it, lose it or even regain it when it does, inevitably get lost? How do you get by with nothing but an intangible force such as belief?

After some time, training and learning the basics, Luke Skywalker is asked to lift his crashed and damaged fighter from the depths of the swamp it is lodged into. He initially questions the request, how can he, a regular looking guy, lift his sunken star fighter from the depths of a swamp with nothing but his mind and something called 'The Force'. He eventually attempts the daunting and surely impossible task and for a second, manages to lift the fighter just a little out of the swamp but then something hits him, possibly doubt and the fighter sinks back in. He proclaims it as impossible. After all, how can something he's never seen done before, be done? The ship is too big, he is too small, it just doesn't add up.

His new master, the wise old Yoda, tells him that size matters not. Yoda himself is old, barely reaches Luke's knees in height and must walk with a stick, yet because he trusts in something intangible because he wholeheartedly believes in it. He can do it. Luke brushes him off again, everything he knows and has already learned goes against the idea of this being possible, he leaves and Yoda sighs. As Luke wanders away with his head down, Yoda closes his eyes and extends his hand.

The fighter lifts from the water and floats with ease over to where Luke is standing, Yoda guiding it along the way. Luke is in awe, even still, he doesn't believe it. Yoda leans in and tells him, "That is why you fail…"

It's such a beautiful scene, it sends chills down my spine every time I watch it and, to me, is the scene that represents a lot of what *Star Wars* on a whole is about. They often present it as hope, the characters mention the word hope, one of the films is literally called *A New Hope* but aren't hope and positive self-belief one and the same?

I don't really think I've given *Star Wars* its proper due. I mentioned it when writing about nostalgia and its power when used well, especially considering the cultural juggernaut it is. But that was more about the behind the scenes, not the powerful themes that made Star Wars the cultural juggernaut it can still be. A prevailing theme across all the characters and stories is hope and belief, the belief of something greater, something that they can't quite see or touch but they just know is waiting. Even when some characters fall into despair or literal darkness, that belief still carries, whether it's in the deepest selves of those characters or passed onto others. Belief never truly dies. That doesn't mean though, that it's an easy task regaining it.

I've already gone over this but following the particular career path I've chosen to follow can be a frequently disheartening affair. There is very little in terms of tangible progress most of the time and it is elusive in the way that you have to find your footing on this path. An optimistic person would remark that a breakthrough or even a significant sign of progress could well be just around the corner but I've turned corner after corner and so far, little seems to have moved, which can prove to be very heavy on the spirit after battling on for so many years. There are plenty of times where I've came very close to giving up on following this path, especially in darker moments but like I've said, something always draws me back and I don't like the idea of thinking about what I might be left with if I give it all up.

It's not just that but a lot of the experiences I've had, which I've already mentioned too many times have left me kind of disheartened and disenchanted with how I should feel. I'm no longer as depressed and feeling as low as I once did, thanks to therapy and all the other help I've received, and I do feel a lot better and comfortable in myself but it's bittersweet in a way. I can't lead that regular life I know some others are more than happy to lead, I've been through too much to act like I can follow along with the norm. It's why I hope this grand endeavour will eventually pay off. I have to believe in this because I struggle to believe in what others find so easy to believe in. It's not an altogether bad place to be in, emotionally and mentally, it's just a lot harder as is going off the beaten path often is. It's also what makes it so hard to regain belief in things that show no signs of becoming better or ideals that others themselves may have lost.

In *The Last Jedi* (Oh, the ever-controversial *Star Wars: The Last Jedi*), the protagonist Rey finds Luke Skywalker alone on an island in the far reaches of the galaxy. The resistance need him to help fight the evil first order and hope he will come back, legend of old to singlehandedly defeat them except he won't, he's a bitter old hermit now, far from the optimistic young hero who lay down his weapon to save his father. He's old and has lost his faith in the good of the galaxy. He is the last Jedi and wants to die that way, taking the last fragments of the order down with him. Rey desperately attempts to convince him otherwise, train her and return to the fight, everybody needs him to come back but Luke doesn't believe that, Luke believes his fighting days are done and that the galaxy is better off without him, especially after his failure led to the creation of the young warrior spearheading the first order.

After Rey leaves him on the island, tired of listening to him not want to re-join the fight, he sets off to burn the last of the Jedi's texts. Bitter and believing wholeheartedly in his failures, he approaches with torch in hand but guess who's there to talk some sense into him? The same old hermit that talked some sense into him back at the beginning of his training. Yoda and Luke talk about failure and what exactly Luke needs to be for the new, young heroes and at the film's finale, he comes back, believing in that sense of hope once again and standing up to the first order. He cements himself as a legend and gives the new resistance something to believe in before passing away as a true legend.

I love *Star Wars* and Luke's journey across the entire saga as I think it's a great example of how belief and hope fades in and out of someone's consciousness. How someone can think they have a hold of it only for it to be destroyed and then reborn in a new light. It's one of the least tangible, yet positive things we can hold onto and even if it takes time to find a grasp on a sense of belief in the moment, sometimes it's the only thing you'll have to keep you going. The rest will just have to come later.

It can take a lot of effort to hold onto just that though when I had no idea if I'd be good enough, I just had to believe I would be just good enough. When I struggle to believe if it will be worth it in the end, I have to believe that my instincts will be right. It's belief or nothing and one of the best parts about Luke Skywalker and *Star Wars* is that it shows that belief is a powerful enough force (Pun Intended) that you and others can accomplish tremendous things when you just hold onto it for that little bit longer. When you take the time to find it again, even when it seems to have all but disappeared from sight, if not for you, then for others.

In the grand finale of the saga, Rey discovers a terrible truth about her lineage and travels to the same island that

Luke exiled himself to with the same intentions of cutting herself off from the galaxy. As she prepares to throw Luke's old sabre into a fiery inferno, his spectral form catches it. His ghost appears to console Rey, as Yoda's ghost did for him. As much as she maybe a danger to everyone, she must go and face down the enemy for the sake of everybody else she must believe that she can do it, that she can win the day. As she prepares to leave, Luke does one last thing to help…she is in need of a ship to travel to her destination and so out of the waters, Luke lifts his old X-Wing fighter. Old Yoda would be proud.

Luke's journey was finally complete. Lifting the fighter from the water wasn't just about giving the hero a way to travel to their destination, and to their fate, it was to give them the belief they needed to face down impossible odds. Yoda lifts it for Luke when he needed it, as does Luke for Rey. That lesson in belief is passed on, lost to all of them and yet, regained by all of them.

There is an important message there about not losing belief or hope as *Star Wars* would categorise it as, which while it's corny and has probably been said a thousand times before is still powerful because cynicism can so easily take over and cause people to just give up, letting go of what they believe in because it's the easier option. This is especially true nowadays when it seems safer to follow the crowd and pick the safest option but belief in something greater isn't something to be thrown away and even if we lose it for a time, it can be regained and reinforced and the sheer power of something so universal can inspire others with wildly different problems and situations. That's how powerful belief can be, our faith in our individual beliefs can be the catalyst for that same force in others.

I've come across so many times when I've wanted to give in, even as recent as writing this, there are times when nothing hopeful seems to be coming of it and it seems like a waste of time and effort but I can never seem able to truly give it up, my belief in a lot of things has changed but my belief in this remains steadfast, even when it feels like I'm staring failure and disappointment in the face. Maybe I just need an old hermit to lift an X-Wing fighter from some water for me...

I must believe. I do believe.

Chapter Eight
Exit Stage Left

Guess what? You've nearly reached the end! That's right. After all that, you've reached the last couple of sections and you'll soon be done. I hope you've enjoyed it. If not, well, then at least you've reached the last stretch that is if you're still here...but I'm sure you are. Right?

To 2019; A strange, uncertain, yet oddly ordinary year.

And now we reach the end. This work has contained a lot of tributes and homages and as a final word I'd like to pay respect to the year 2019 because 2019 has been an interesting year. It's been a fairly ordinary year where everything has formed its own pattern of contentment, yet it could also be an interesting year in how it affects everything going forward. It's kind of like a foundational year, one where I've taken stock of things and looked back at the past as well as trying to plan for the best kind of future I can hope for. Chapters have closed, things have come full circle and I hope it leads to something better.

As I've gone over, it's been a sort of swansong for a lot of aspects of my life in a way that no other year has. I'm nearly 25, so I guess I'll have reached the quarter point in my life soon and I hope that everything I've strived for over the past decade and maybe longer comes to fruition sooner rather than later.

But as far as years ago, it's not been bad compared to the rest it's been a pretty stable year. Nothing incredible or tragic has happened but I guess I didn't want it to. I just wanted to work on goals and problems that have been gnawing away for some time. For the most part I've accomplished what I set out to accomplish this year, closing the book on things that I'm prepared to let go of and finishing goals and objectives that have perhaps lingered for too long. Looking back over the year, some of the stuff I've accomplished may come off as miniscule or irrelevant to most people but different things mean more to others than some.

If the year has been productive but ordinary, it definitely has a sense of uncertainty to it. Going beyond this year and into the next decade, the pressure is mounting to get on with other things in life. I've gone over the fact that I'm not quite as far ahead as others when it comes to the more adult aspects of life and the clock's ticking on that, as much as I might wish it wasn't. It feels like as much as I want to achieve long held ambitions, I may be heading into the last chance saloon. I've worked out a pretty good system for working on and balancing a lot of aspects to suit my needs.

So, there is definitely an uncertainty about going forward into the New Year more than ever. This year being a culmination of my own efforts and the general feeling surrounding it has given me the feeling that life is either preparing me for a grand triumph of goals or another moment where I'm left disappointed. I hope, as many others probably would, that it's the former that prevails. That all my talk of being persistent in your dreams and believing in your individual talents and characteristics will pay off in the most joyous of ways. It'll be interesting looking back on this work later on in life and seeing just how things turned out. I could end up reading this again with a feeling of either warmth or bitterness, I'll just have to wait and see…

Whatever happens though, I have to say I'm grateful for the events of this year, and the time and patience I've been given by life and by the people I know, to at least attempt to do something different and to do something more than what I've ended up with. I'm happy that I've had time to reflect on the past and be able to look at events with a calmer mind. Less volatile in my emotions, I can see things with more balance and be able to get a better handle on why and turn to other things instead.

Either way, with all the past experience, it's difficult not to look on with a sense of dread. As much as I try and be more optimistic in my thoughts and my approach, I still find it hard not to step very slowly into the future, hoping that it doesn't bite like it has done so many times in the past. Life feels like a far cry from what it was like in the first 12 or so years and I hope that maybe it will turn around again, after all this time and effort, I'll be able to breathe easy.

This year, I've repaired relationships, written and re-written everything I've wanted to write and ultimately done what I've needed to be able to accept any great change I'll have to go through in the coming years. I mentioned that I considered 2019 to be a foundational year. It feels like I'm ready to cross a threshold, only I'm stood right in it. Looking back on the past and spending time appreciating what I always enjoyed while at the same time, working on the building blocks of what my preferred future might be. A part of me doesn't want to cross that threshold, even if it ends up being the best future I could possibly imagine. They always say it's about the journey, not the destination and now that I've come to appreciate the journey and what it's taken to get to this point, I almost don't want it to end.

But I can't hang around in limbo forever, I know I have a chance to achieve something dear to my heart, it's written right here after all. I just don't want to lose some of the things I've come to enjoy so much. Whatever happens in the future, I hope that the best of all worlds can come together and finally create something where I can happily settle down and live a life I truly enjoy. I just hope that for all my grandiose beliefs and ambitions, the effort will all be worth it. For someone who has spent a lot of his life, anxiously trying to predict what can and might happen, I hope life might surprise me again.

I also have one last promise to fulfil. A promise I made to myself when I first started down this path. Way back when I first took my love of fiction and merged it with my love of creative writing, I made a promise to myself that I'd never give up. No matter what, I'd push on through whatever attempted to waylay me from something that meant more to me than I can explain. That 12-year-old boy cemented that promise in their heart and mind in the hopes that, in the future, near or far, they would break down whatever wall necessary to achieve that goal. Nearing 25 years old and with 2020 looming on the horizon, maybe I can fulfil that promise I made to myself over a decade ago.

Somewhere in the past, there's a 12-year-old boy counting on it.

A small acknowledgment to the book and its writer who helped me to realise I could write something like this.

Before I began writing this, even before I began thinking about doing something like what you've been reading and hopefully enjoying. I was reading a brilliant book. It's called *Creativity Inc.* and it was written by Ed Catmull, one of the founding members of that magical company we all know as Pixar. I've mentioned them multiple times already, between *Toy Story* and *The Incredibles*, as well as the other films they've made, they have always told stories that resonated with me, as well as countless others.

It was only after I finished reading it in about three days flat, which is ridiculously fast for me, that I had the idea of writing my own thoughts down. Which in turn, led to this. So, as an acknowledgment to Mr Catmull and his wonderfully inspiring book, I want to repeat something he put at the end of his own book. A series of summaries and diatribes on the points he's made and other small notes that maybe didn't end up being substantial enough to write large sections about but are still important, nonetheless.

Thank you, Ed Catmull, your company and its stories continue to inspire me, even when it's about the foundations which led to those very stories.

-   Keep on Climbing that Hill

Sometimes, all you can do is just push on. You may have wildly differing beliefs and goals to others and are struggling to put them into practice, into a solid state. During those times, the only thing you can really do is keep going. It's difficult because the easy way out, whatever it may be, is always available. You can bend to fit everybody else's view and plan but if you have a core belief that you are passionate about, then keep going. People aren't kidding when they say it's about the journey and not the destination, sometimes it's all about the effort you put in getting to that triumphant moment that means the difference between succeeding or not. You may tumble down the hill in many different ways, sometimes it's failure, sometimes you just get waylaid but the most important thing if you want to truly succeed is that you keep on climbing that hill.

-   Remember who you are

It's easy to get lost in life. It's easy to follow others ways because of fear of not fitting in or that you don't quite know what to do but if you take the time and prepare for the uncomfortable feelings it may bring, you can find out what your core beliefs, characteristics and traits are. Once you have found your centre, you will be able to live a much more peaceful and fulfilling life because you will know exactly what you like, don't like and so on. You will be less easily swayed by external forces and will find it easier to go on, knowing you know yourself at a much deeper level. Even if you do lose that sense of self, anyone can find it again under the right circumstances. Remembering who you are is often the key to getting back on the correct path.

- **Appreciate the Quiet**

The world is now a much more interconnected place and is much more attuned to social people, especially with the internet and all the different social media apps and sites. It's easier to keep in contact with almost everybody and so expectation has increased to be always there, always ready to respond. In light of this, don't forget to take those silent moments. A walk somewhere secluded can do wonders, especially when the world becomes overwhelming as it can be in the modern age but most of all, appreciate it. Appreciate the simplicity of what you notice, and remember, that it's OK to disappear for a moment every now and then.

- **Different isn't Wrong**

Speaking of our more interconnected world, it's also much easier to go along with the crowd to follow everybody else. It's a little harder to be open about your individual characteristics and hobbies. Especially when there seems to be an ingrained way of doing things, in my experience anyway, it's important to not shut away your stranger, differing aspects for the sake of fitting in. A funny example is music, my choice in music is the orchestral scores to films, shows and games, a lot of people find that strange but that's the music I love most. We all have our place but our place rests on us finding our true selves, even if that may be a lot different to what others expect.

- One eye on the Past

It's important to remember our history, personal and communal, so we don't repeat the mistakes of those before us. Some people find it easy to move on from their past and it is often encouraged to 'throw off the shackles of the past' but I think it's better to accept whatever that past may be, so you can learn from it, use it to inform whatever decisions you need to make in the present. Some people's past may be unfortunately tragic or upsetting but if you can find the strength to look at that past, it may prove invaluable later on down the line. The past, present and future are all equally important, as much as we may want to push forward for that greater future.

- There is always a Choice

One phrase that both of my therapists used was 'There is always a choice', I found this intriguing because as far as I know, my therapists never corresponded with each other and even if they did, a small detail like that would never be that important to pass on. It's stuck with me because I believe it holds more power than people realise. There is always a choice in every single situation, even those that are normally dictated by right or wrong. Right or wrong are good indicators and yet they are often impulsive in their nature. When someone does something that upsets you, it may be 'right' to address that with anger but there is always a choice. I've used this phrase to inform a few of my own decisions since therapy and have found that it's been quite useful. Times when I could have responded with anger or frustration because it was the immediate reaction have turned out differently because I realised I have the final choice in my response. I decide to be patient and calm, it's served me well. So, in any situation, remember, you always have a choice.

- **Be Kind**

It's sappy, stupid, overly sentimental and I know you've heard it a million times before but in this day and age I think it can't be said enough that we should all be kind to the people we interact with. I see and hear a lot of negativity thrown around, even in small conversation and it's unfortunate because as I've said, we all have a choice. Choose to be kind, even if all that means is that you stop saying that bad thing you were about to say. Lend a helping hand, give someone a compliment, I know it's corny and overdone. Just be kind.

- **Don't Sweat the Small Stuff**

This is a bit rich coming from someone with anxiety and a dash of OCD but people get so caught up in tiny problems sometimes. Plenty of folks argue about the smallest of issues that any other time would be stupid and trivial. I used to worry and panic over inconsequential details all the time, I still do on days that are a little too exhausting for my mind but at the end of the day how much of it really matters? Not everything is worthy of mention, let alone conflict. So don't sweat it.

- **Life is stupid but beautiful**

I get that life can sometimes feel like it's pelting you with every handful of mud it's got and like I once did, it can make you feel like there's nothing else to it. Just one bad day after another, so, yes, life is stupid but it's also beautiful (I know we're getting really sappy in this last section) and sometimes all that means is something incredibly simple. One stupid little thing I like to do is look up at night. I was at an event once, a party or something, and it was full, everybody was having fun and having a great time. Me being the quiet and insular person I was, stood outside and looked up. My entire vision became filled with nothing but stars and the space between them. I might as well have been up there with them. By some circumstance, it calmed me down. I'll often do it now when I get back home at night, just look up at the stars. Life's complications fade away and I just observe the stars for a minute. Life is stupid but also beautiful.

- **Safety is not Happiness**

Often confused and misinterpreted, after long periods of struggle and effort, people can often attribute that feeling of safety to a similar longing of happiness. Safety is fine and a worthy goal to aim for and sustain but sometimes that feeling of safety can fade or be irrelevant to others in terms of what they need out of life. It can be tricky to discern but sometimes it's right to question whether safety equates to happiness.

- Balance is Key

It's only become apparent to me in the past couple of years but it's imperative that you find the correct balance for your own individual life. This can be harder than you think, especially with the constant changes that happen. This makes real balance more like constantly tending to spinning plates than achieving a non-moving entity. A non-moving entity will eventually stagnate and then balance will have to be achieved from scratch. Balance changes as much as anything else in life and you have to work with it.

- Take your Time

There always seems to be a rush to hit those goals, especially those cornerstones of life that nearly everybody will eventually achieve but these cornerstones often bring with them a large degree of responsibility and need attentive care to be nurtured properly and effectively. Don't rush. Some people aim to get to these lofty goals before they're truly ready and eventually, it comes back to haunt them in one way or another. There's never been a race to achieve these goals, so don't treat it as such, allow the right moment to make its way to you. Then leap.

- Be the Wizard

Remember in *The Hobbit* when Bilbo Baggins is living his perfectly normal life, content and happy. Then the wizard Gandalf comes knocking at his door and whisks him away on an adventure involving dragons, treasure and great battles. I read a comment from someone saying that they wished a wizard would take them on an adventure, someone else responded with 'Why can't you be the Wizard'? It's a good point, we often expect someone else to rescue us from drudgery rather than ourselves. It works in more ways than that though, expecting someone else to do the work? Expecting someone else to be kinder? Expecting someone else to say the first good word? Don't wait, don't complain. Dude, just be the Wizard.

Well, I hope I managed to get everything down. I'm sure there's bound to be one thing I remember when it's too late but I'd say most of it's in there.

I guess the only thing left to say is thank you for reading. I hope that it has been an enjoyable read most of all, I know that not everybody may agree with what I've said across these pages but at the very least I hope that you had a good time reading through it. If you happened to find it insightful, that it has made you think on some things, then all the better. Maybe in another 25 years, when I'm edging close to 50, I'll write another like this that looks back over that time. But for now, I'll just hope that after what has felt like a very long winded and exhausting journey that I'm finally given the chance to live out what I've always wanted to do.

It's been an interesting time, this first quarter of my life, especially the past 12 or so years. Ever since I first heard that my parents would no longer be together, when all of this really started, it's been an interesting journey that has unfortunately, often been more emotionally draining and darker than I would have liked. But maybe, after going through and learning, an awful lot I'll be able to finally stand on the peak of that metaphorical hill and take a relieved breath.

I hope that with everything coming into retrospect and many a strand finally coming full circle, I'll finally turn that elusive corner that's evaded me for so long.

So thank you and hopefully, someday soon, you'll hear from me again.